Adaptations of Desert Organisms

Edited by J.L. Cloudsley-Thompson

R.T. Wilson

Ecophysiology of the Camelidae and Desert Ruminants

With 37 Figures

Springer-Verlag Berlin Heidelberg New York
London Paris Tokyo Hong Kong

Dr. Richard Trevor Wilson
Bartridge House
Umberleigh
North Devon EX37 9AS
United Kingdom

Cover illustration: photograph by J.L. Cloudsley-Thompson

ISBN 3-540-50806-6 Springer-Verlag Berlin Heidelberg New York
ISBN 0-387-50806-6 Springer-Verlag New York Berlin Heidelberg

Library of Congress Cataloging-in-Publication Data. Wilson, R.T. Ecophysiology of the Camelidae and desert ruminants / R.T. Wilson. p. cm. – (Adaptations of desert organisms) Bibliography: p. 104. Includes index. ISBN 0-387-50806-6 (U.S.: alk. paper) 1. Ruminants. 2. Camelidae. 3. Desert fauna. I. Title. II. Series. QL 737.U5W54 1989 599.73'5041'09154–dc20

© Springer-Verlag Berlin Heidelberg 1989

Printed in the United States of America

Typesetting: Fotosatz & Design, Berchtesgaden

2131/3145-543210 – Printed on acid-free paper

This is again for Mary, who still does not stand and wait,
and for Andrew, who now willingly serves.
And for Azeb, Selamawit and Astier, who make life easier.

Preface

I have spent less time in the arid zone in the last few years than I did during the 1960's, 1970's and early 1980's. This results from a progression through age and a career structure which gradually shifted the emphasis of my work from being essentially field-oriented to essentially office-bound.

When, therefore, I was asked by John Cloudsley-Thompson to undertake the writing of this book I hesitated for two reasons. One reason was that, although I now had access to good library facilities and kept up with the literature on the arid zones and their fauna, I was not sure that a sedentary and pleasant life in a temperate highland island in tropical Africa would provide a mental attitude suitable to writing a book which related to areas where life is usually nomadic and often extremely disagreeable. The other reason was that I was uncertain whether I could devote the time necessary to researching and writing the book on top of my professional (which now specifically excluded research in the arid zones and on camels) and social (new-found and time-consuming) commitments.

In the event I accepted and the fates were kind to me. By some peculiar combination of circumstances I was given the opportunity to spend a considerable part of the first half of 1988 in some of the driest areas of the globe. I had already visited all of the locations used for the construction of Fig. 2.2 except for Swakopmund in Namibia during the course of earlier peregrinations. The Government of Sudan, the Food and Agriculture Organisation and the World Bank all considered my presence in some part of the arid zones to be a necessity during early 1988.

This book largely results from those visits. Not only is it about animals that live in the driest zones of the world: it was mainly written in those zones.

Sudan, Morocco, Niger, Kenya, Ethiopia
Summer 1989   R.T. WILSON

Contents

1 Introduction

Classic physiology studies have rarely taken the environment in which an animal lives into account. As a result, little has been gleaned of the evolutionary pressures which have made animals more or less fit for the environments in which they are currently found. Comparative physiology has attempted to extend studies away from humans and from some of the more easily accessible domestic and laboratory animals in an effort to understand some aspects of organisation which would not be possible in humans and their familiar animals. Comparative physiology, however, has thus far, as pure physiology, taken little, if any, cognisance of the evolutionary and adaptive aspects of development.

The aims of ecophysiology – and it is not the intention here to attempt to distinguish this discipline from environmental physiology or physiological ecology – are to define the adaptive features of an organism which fit it to its environment. It is presumed that such adaptations result from stress, and therefore that the environment in which the animal lives is a difficult one. Adaptation is not, however, restricted to physiological mechanisms, and these are often intimately associated with anatomical and, particularly, behavioural adaptations. Each of these characters reinforces the others and it is therefore often difficult to distinguish which adaptations are contributing most to an organism's ability to survive and thrive in a difficult environment.

The study of adaptation to stress is a relatively recent phenomenon. One of the first books to be published in the general field (Buxton 1923) dates back some 60 years. It was not, however, until after the Second World War (when technical advances in biometeorology and in the ability to provide artificially controlled environments within fine limits had been made) that studies of adaptations to stress became more general. It is, of course, difficult to simulate the real environment in the laboratory. Conversely, in the field it is not always possible, indeed it is most unusual, to be able to control variables. In the laboratory all variables except the one under study can be held constant. The difficulties encountered in the field have thus sometimes led to a distinction being made between ecophysiology and physiological ecology on the one hand, which are based mainly on studies made in the natural environment, and environmental physiology on the other hand, where studies are made mainly in the laboratory.

Be that as it may, by the middle of the 1960's a number of groups of workers throughout the world had done sufficient work on adaptive physiology to be able to produce books dealing with this general area (Kleiber 1961; Macfarlane 1964; Schmidt-Nielsen 1964; Folk 1966) and a number of landmark papers had also been published (Leitch and Thompson 1945; Schmidt-Nielsen et al. 1956, 1957a; Payne and Hutchinson 1963; Schoen 1969; Taylor 1970a, b). A decade later, adaptation of animals to their environment was "à la mode" and was the subject of numerous conferences and collections of papers (Maloiy 1972a; Yousef, Horvath and Bullard 1972; Hadley 1975; Goodall, Perry and Howes 1979).

It will have become evident from the references just cited that stress on animals, at least as considered by man, is more prevalent in deserts than elsewhere. Stress is also exerted on animals in mountain and arctic areas. The references quoted relate mostly to vertebrate mammals and more specifically to ungulates. Adaptation is not, however, restricted to these taxa. Adaptation may, indeed, be better developed in other animal groups and much of our understanding has come from reptiles (for a recent comprehensive text see Bradshaw 1986), from insects and other arthropods (Edney 1971; Hadley 1972; Hamilton and Seely 1976) as well as from birds (Marder 1973; Louw, Belonje and Coetzee 1969; Bartholomew, White and Howell 1976; Dixon and Louw 1978) and from other classes such as Amphibia and Pisces. Some behavioural mechanisms, which were initially thought to be adaptations to the environment, for example the building of a huge enclosed nest by the African endemic bird, the hamerkop, do not seem to serve any such function (Wilson and Wilson 1986, 1989; Wilson 1989). Adaptations to stress by plants are also very varied and well developed.

Some of the major adaptations exhibited by desert organisms (Louw and Seely 1982) are:

- Size and shape;
- Orientation to the sun to reduce profile area exposed to the heat source;
- Colour and nature of the integument;
- Absorption and storage of water;
- Facultative breeding or reproduction;
- Tolerance of high temperatures and tissue dehydration;
- Specialised respiratory patterns;
- Conservation of water, in particular by reducing urine flow, excreting drier faeces and concentrating nitrogen and other electrolytes;
- Reduction in metabolic rate;
- Modifications in digestive physiology;
- Escape or retreat to more favourable sites (for example rodents and other small animals living in burrows).

The major physiological adaptations (as opposed to morphological, anatomical or behavioural ones with which they may be intimately linked) can be considered to fall into three major categories. Water balance is perhaps the most important of the three and is adjusted or controlled by means of: evaporative cooling by panting and sweating; tolerance of water loss and the capacity to reduce body mass by water loss without this affecting other vital functions; variation in glomerular filtration rates, adjustment of renal plasma flow and urine flow; reduction of the water content of faeces so that they can be excreted in a more solid form; and, when the opportunity arises, water can be ingested quickly and in large quantities. Thermal relationships are also important, the most common means of temperature control being: facultative hyperthermia during the day and hypothermia at night, animals capable of doing this being in effect bradymetabolic; counter-current heat exchange; and the nature of the skin and coat providing protection against heat loss or gain. Finally, nutritional adaptations are related to: the physiology of nutrition in part related to the ability to select the most nourishing food from the total available; the ability to build up reserves in the form of fat; and reducing food and water requirements through a lowered metabolic rate.

Following a chapter on the desert environment, all of these three major adaptive characters will be considered in detail.

2 Deserts and the Desert Environment

Deserts are amongst the most stressful environments in the world. They present enormous challenges for both plant and animal life at the cell, organism and population levels. Deserts are typically associated with extreme temperature and extreme aridity. Solar radiation is usually intense and wind can impose additional stress. Food and water are often in short supply and, because the vegetation is sparse, there may be little or no shade.

2.1 Climate

A peculiar feature of deserts is the rapidity with which changes occur in environmental parameters. These changes may occur diurnally or seasonally but they impose additional stress and require further adaptations from animals and plants. Temperatures, for example, may differ by more than 50° C from day to night and an absolute deficiency of food may rapidly turn to superabundance very shortly after rain has fallen. Although usually associated especially by the layman, with sandy areas, desert soils are of very diverse genesis in different areas. Soil type affects not only water holding capacity and thus the length of the period during which vegetative growth is possible but also the kinds of plants which will grow. As an example of the latter there might be saline or non-saline food available, the former posing additional problems in use and conversion.

The term desert is, however, an inexact one. The most characteristic feature of such an area is the overall moisture deficit and the markedly seasonal nature of its supply. Within these definitions it is possible to find "desert" areas with rainfall varying from zero in many years to areas which regularly receive as much as 600mm per year distributed over one or two short 2 to 4 month periods. On an annual basis, evapotranspiration is always more, and usually is greatly in excess of, precipitation. For short periods of the year, or for short periods in some years, rainfall might nonetheless exceed water loss, and vegetative growth is possible. It needs to be noted that vegetative growth is not always related immediately to precipitation and may occur after a period of weeks or months has elapsed since a combination of favourable conditions, as in the case of the 'gizu' of the southern Sahara (Wilson 1978).

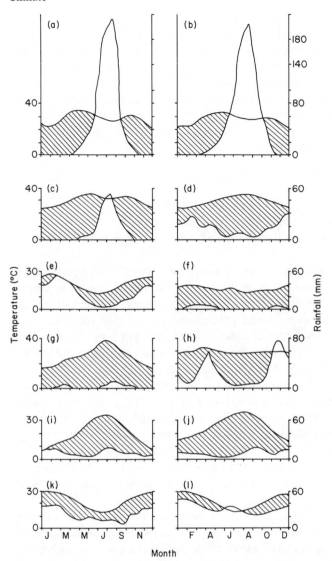

Fig. 2.1. Ombrothermic diagrams for some typical desert locations (Africa: *(a)* Zinder 13°48'N 08°59'E 510 m; *(b)* Niono 13°58'N 5°55'W270 m; *(c)* Khartoum 15°36'N 32°32'E 380 m; *(d)* Massawa 15°37'N 39°27'E 20 m; *(e)* Tsabong 26°03'S 22°27'E 962 m; *(f)* Swakopmund 22°41'S 14°31'E 12 m; *(g)* Tindouf 27°43'N 08°08'E 600 m; *(h)* Garissa 00°29'S 39°38'E 128 m. America: *(i)* Las Vegas 36°10'N 115°10'W648 m; *(j)* Yuma 32°40'N 114°39'W 59 m. Australia: *(k)* Alice Springs 23°49'S 133°53'E 545 m; *(l)* Bourke 30°05'S 145°57'E 108 m)

Various measures of aridity, other than a simple measure of rainfall, have been proposed to describe the semi-arid zone (600–400mm rainfall per year), the arid zone (400–100mm) and the hyper-arid zone (100mm). Early attempts to classify the degree of aridity were based on potential and actual rates of evapotranspiration (Thornthwaite 1948) and on modifications of this method (Meigs 1952). A commonly used measure of aridity and one which lends itself to a simplified visual presentation in the form of ombrothermic diagrams (Fig. 2.1) is the Xerothermic Index of Bagnouls and Gaussen 1953; 1957). The xerothermic index is calculated as:

$$X = K(N-n) - E[b+r]/2$$

in which   X is the index
               K is the coefficient of relative humidity
               N is the number of dry days per month
and   n, b and r are days of rain, fog and dew per month.

Ombrothermic diagrams are constructed from precipitation and temperature figures where P in millimetres is graphed against t in degrees centigrade (on a scale equal to twice the same value as precipitation). Dry periods are defined as those where precipitation is less than the figure of 2t. It is also possible to construct climatograms of different types from primary meteorological data which also convey the likely levels of stress in relation to precipitation, temperature and humidity (Fig. 2.2).

A more simple and practical measure of aridity uses the simple ratio P/ETP, where P is annual precipitation in mm and ETP is the mean annual potential evapotranspiration also in mm. This classification, which has been adopted by some technical agencies of the United Nations (Riquier and Rossetti 1976; MAB 1979) – and will probably therefore assume wide currency – defines the arid zone as a region in which the ratio P/ETP falls between 0.20 and 0.03 and the hyper-arid zone as being one where the ratio is less than 0.03.

None of the classifications discussed takes into account the effects of wind and insolation. Wind can be important not only in its effects on evapotranspiration but also directly in relation to comfort. An indication of the importance accorded to wind by humans who inhabit desert areas can be gained from the names given to them: 'habub' in Sudan; 'harmattan' in West Africa; 'khamsin' (the wind that blows for 50 days) in Mediterranean North Africa and the Middle East; 'simoon' in Iran; and 'berg' in Namibia. Noy-Meir (1973) has, however, insisted that water is the most important factor in desert environments (because it is absolutely low, highly variable in time and space, and is largely unpredictable with coefficients of variation of 100%) and that its use as the principal descriptive factor is the most logical and pragmatic.

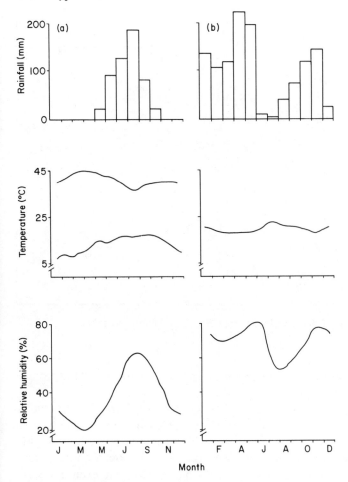

Fig. 2.2. Climatograms of (a) a desert area compared with (b) a situation where climatic features are relatively constant

2.2 Desert Types and Locations

The location of the major deserts in the world is shown in Fig. 2.3. Most deserts lie within or just outside the tropics. In these areas they also tend to be situated on the western side of the relative land masses, close to oceans with cold currents, or in the interiors of continents. It has been postulated (McGinnies 1979) that three general causes can act, singly or in combination, to produce an arid climate. These causes are: physical distance or topographical impedance of an area from oceanic moisture; the presence of large and stable high pressure air masses which resist convective currents; and a

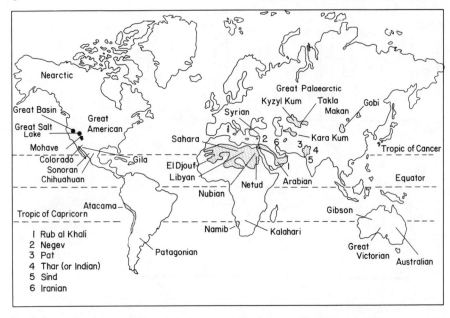

Fig. 2.3. The location of the world's deserts (Cloudsley-Thompson 1977)

lack of storm systems which would create an unstable environment and provide the uplift necessary for precipitation to occur.

The second cause is perhaps the most classic one and is particularly responsible for the formation of the major subtropical deserts. As can be seen from Fig. 2.3, these are also the regions where the majority of the world's hyper-arid areas are found. The stable air masses result from the trade winds which, in both hemispheres, blow towards the equator, gathering moisture as they proceed. This causes them to rise and be subject to adiabatic cooling close to the equator. These cooled air masses condense and precipitation occurs. As a result, the high alitude winds moving away from the equator are relatively dry. This high altitude air mass eventually descends into the high-pressure regions of the sub-tropics and becomes compressed and heated as it does so, with a further concomitant reduction in humidity. These causal factors have given rise to a general model of the world's deserts (Cloudsley-Thompson 1977) which is described in Table 2.1. Other models of desert types have been proposed and it would also be possible to include factors other than climate in the classification. Such factors could include altitude – which might affect precipitation and would certainly influence temperature – soil type, and vegetation. The last is a resultant of rainfall and soil type. Soil types appear to be less variable and less rich in nutrients in the Australian deserts than elsewhere as a consequence of low soil nitrogen and phosphorus status due to a long history of weathering.

Table 2.1. A classification of the world's deserts

Type	Location	Examples	Principal formative causes	Temperature
Sub-tropical	Within and just outside tropics: 30°S–30°N	Sahara (sensu lato) Arabian Kalahari Somali/Kenya Australian	High pressure air masses along each side of the tropics	Hot Hot Hot Hot Hot
Cool coastal	Western sides of land masses in proximity to cold ocean currents	Namib Atacama Baja California	High pressure air masses, intensified by near presence of cold currents or by advective fog	Hot-cool, climate ameliorated somewhat by cool on-shore winds
Rain shadow	On leeward side of mountain ranges	Patagonia Mohave Great Basin Australia	Windward sides of mountains cause air to rise, cool adiabatically and precipitate moisture. Lee-side air masses are therefore dry.	Cold Hot Hot Hot
Interior continental	At interior of large continental land masses between major wind belts and associated storm systems	Central Australian North American Central Asian	Large dry air masses at long distances from major sources of moisture	Hot Hot Cold

This history of weathering raises the question of the long-term stability of desert environments. A well-known and well documented example of long-term change is that of the Sahara, where several different factors, including prehistoric industries, soil type changes, vegetation components and patterns, and climate, have enabled a reconstruction of events over the past 10000 years to be made (Quezel 1965). At about 10000 years before present (BP) the central Sahara climate was arid and vegetation was of the steppe type with some fragmented Mediterranean incursions. Approximately 2000 years later the climate had become temperate and Mediterranean sub-humid to humid in type, which allowed the establishment of mixed, mainly deciduous forests in the mountain massifs with coniferous Aleppo pine forests predominating at lower altitudes. At 6000 BP the climate was again becoming dry although still relatively moist at altitude and the Mediterranean flora persisted with the addition of olives, heather and some other species. By about 3000 years BP the climate changed fundamentally from a Mediterranean type with rainfall in the winter to a Sahel type with summer rainfall, the Mediterranean vegetation subsequently disappearing to be replaced, in the main, by *Acacia* species. In the last 2000 years the climate has become gradually drier and, except in some favoured areas, the vegetation has disappeared almost completely. Some of these favoured areas which still contain remnants of the original vegetation are the massifs of Ennedi and Tibesti in the central Sahara and the Adrar n'Iforas, the Aïr and Jebel Marra along the southern fringes (Williams and Faure 1980).

The boundaries of the deserts with non-desert areas are subject to various climatic influences. The major subtropical deserts have steppic or "bush" vegetation types on the boundaries closest to the equator, resulting largely from the summer rainfall regime. On the boundaries farthest from the equator the climate of most of these deserts is of the Mediterranean type with winter rainfall and summer drought. The vegetation is principally of the sclero-phyllous brush type associated with the Mediterranean sub-humid (800–600mm rainfall) and humid types (1200–800mm) of climate. These vegetative associations are known as 'macquis' and 'garigue' in southern Europe and along the Mediterranean littoral of north Africa, 'macchia' in South Africa, 'mulga' and 'malee' in Australia and 'chaparral' in the United States.

The major interior continental deserts are usually cold at the margins farthest from the equator, as are the rain shadow deserts. This is mainly because cold polar air masses can arrive in the winter without being hindered by large mountain ranges between the poles and the deserts themselves.

Cool coastal deserts are essentially extensions of the major subtropical arid regions but, as already stated, are influenced by cold ocean currents: the Benguela in the case of the Namib; the Humboldt in South America; and the California in North America. Temperature inversions in these deserts cause advectional fogs which are often the main source of moisture.

The Sahara is by far the most arid and largest of the world's deserts, although it is slightly more humid at its western extremity than at its centre and in the east. In North Africa it is estimated that 5323000km^2 are desert of which about 90% is hyper-arid, and desert covers 93% of the whole region. Australia has about 6328000km^2 of desert but none of this is hyper-arid, about 65% is arid and 35% semi-arid, while 80% of the total land area is desert (Le Houérou 1979). Asia has by far the largest desert area of any continent (16477000km^2) of which about only 6% is hyper-arid, about 48 per cent is arid and the remainder semi-arid, but the total of desert areas covers only 38% of the region. In North and South America 25 and 20% respectively of the total area are desert, but less than 1% of this is hyper-arid in North America and only about 6% is hyper-arid in South America: in both continents semi-arid areas are greater in area than arid ones, in North America the semi-arid zone covering about 65% of all so-called desert areas (Monod 1973).

2.3   Life in Deserts

High temperatures and low precipitation result in the aridity which poses the major problem to survival of both plants and animals in deserts.

Plants have adopted various strategies to resist aridity and to take advantage of the ephemeral availability of better conditions. Adaptive strategies include specialised root systems, modifications of the cuticle, modifications to the size and shape of the leaves, and orientation of the whole plant or of parts of it in line with the sun to reduce the heat load. A major strategy adopted by animals, that of movement, is not usually available to plants. Perhaps as an alternative, plants have, in many cases, become ephemeral. Many desert plants, particularly in the tropical deserts, also use the C_4 pathway and are thereby able to sustain very rapid photosynthesis during the short favourable growing period.

The stresses imposed by heat and aridity can be reduced to a considerable extent if these two factors can be avoided or their effects lessened by behavioural mechanisms. Small forms of animal life (arthropods, reptiles and small mammals, especially rodents) could be subject to considerably greater problems than larger animals, not only because size confers some advantages in stress adaptation but also because conditions are more extreme near the ground than farther away from it. The soil at ground level heats and cools very rapidly. At Khartoum in Sudan the annual mean soil temperature at 1cm depth fluctuates from less than 20° C just before sunrise to a maximum of 65° C in the early afternoon (Oliver 1965). At depth, because of the insulating properties of soil, both diurnal and, to a lesser extent seasonal, fluctuations are reduced. At 50cm the diurnal variation becomes very much attenuated and at 100cm it may be reduced to a very narrow range so that the temperature at this depth is almost stable. Animals which can construct burrows or make use of natural crevices in the soil therefore have the opportunity of escaping from the most severe effects of heat.

Other escape mechanisms include aestivation (involving a long period of dormancy or torpor in which metabolic rate and body temperature may be considerably reduced by physiological mechanisms) and, of course, migration. Migration is, in practice, restricted to large mammals and birds whilst aestivation is an escape method adopted by small mammals and bradymetabolic animals. Some authors have suggested that as the process of aestivation is not the same in tachymetabolic as in bradymetabolic animals, different terminology should be used. Classic examples of long migrations include the case of the springbok (*Antidorcas marsupialis*) in southern Africa. Shorter migrations include that of the gemsbok (*Oryx gazella*) in the Kalahari desert of Namibia and Botswana.

Recent texts have attempted to distinguish between "escape" and "retreat" from the desert environment (Louw and Seely 1982). Escape is considered to be a longer-term effect whilst retreat is of a short-term nature, often occurring diurnally, with or without circadian torpor. Retreat is more common in arthropods, reptiles and small mammals than in large mammals. Where conditions are favourable, however, large mammals will adopt retreat tactics such as shade-seeking during the heat of the day and/or restricting feeding and other activities to night periods or when the sky is overcast.

3 Temperature and Heat Relations

3.1 Introduction

All mammals are primarily tachymetabolic or homeothermic animals. In general, tachymetaboly requires a more or less strict control of body temperature within rather fine limits. These limits – the "comfort zone" – vary among different species. Within the comfort zone an animal does not have to expend energy to maintain a stable temperature. The preferred body temperature of most mammals at rest is usually within the range of 36° C to 38° C. In an individual animal the temperature may vary considerably at any one time, usually being most constant in the deep body or "core" and varying, either hotter or colder, at the surface and at the extremities.

Mammals gain heat from three sources. These sources are metabolic heat from the oxidation of food, radiant heat from the sun and the surrounding air, and convected heat from the soil surface. The principal sources of heat gain for an animal are shown in Fig. 3.1. For larger mammals subject to continual exposure to the sun and unable to retreat from it, the strongest source of heat is associated with solar radiation, both direct short wave and

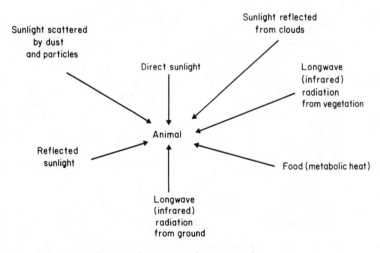

Fig. 3.1. The radiant environment of a mammal

various forms of reflected long wave radiation. The amount of radiation absorbed depends on a number of factors, including the area exposed to the different sources of heat and on the characteristics of the skin or coat. Short wave radiation, for example, is reflected better by light than by dark coats but long wave radiation is almost totally absorbed, irrespective of the colour of. the coat.

Thermal equilibrium is achieved in most animals through a continuous antagonistic process of heat gain and heat loss. Thermoregulation in mammals is almost inextricably related with water metabolism (Fig. 3.2). Heat gains from the sun, from the other components of the radiant environment and from the metabolic heat produced by the oxidation of food are balanced by heat loss through re-radiation from the coat, by convection and conduction, and by cutaneous and respiratory evaporation of water. In some mammals, heat can be stored temporarily or excess heat evacuated by raising or lowering the temperature above or below the physiological norm.

Animals adapted to extremes of climate often have the ability to allow their temperatures to fluctuate between rather wide limits. This extended range probably results from a seasonal or longer-term acclimatization and from genetic adaptations. Strictly speaking, animals with this characteristic of extended temperature range are bradymetabolic rather than tachyme-

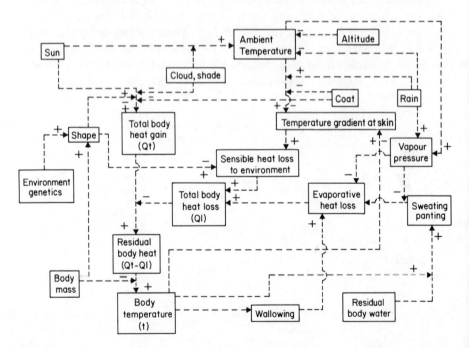

Fig. 3.2. Factors affecting the environmental heat load and thermoregulation in mammals (King 1983)

tabolic. Bradymetaboly may consist of hyperthermy in which the body temperature is in excess of the ambient, or hypothermy, where it is below the ambient. The actual range is species-specific. The benefits of hyperthermia are a reduction in the amount of heat gained (because of the smaller difference in the temperature gradient between the animal and its environment) and savings of both water and energy through a lowered need for evaporative cooling.

The extent to which animals can vary their temperatures depends on body size, the water balance and individual metabolism. Animals of different mass adopt different methods. Large mammals with low area-to-weight ratios and low weight-specific metabolic rates exhibit a slow rise in body temperature during the day from low night-time levels. The time during which evaporation must finally be resorted to in order to control body temperature can thus be significantly reduced or even eliminated for longer or shorter periods. Small mammals, with less favourable ratios of surface area to body mass heat up much more quickly and may have to employ physical (radiation and convection) and physiological mechanisms much sooner and for longer periods than is the case for larger mammals.

Hyperthermia is usually facultative. In this case it will only be resorted to when water is in short supply or the state of dehydration of the animal demands that water be conserved efficiently. Reduced metabolic rates during hyperthermia assist in increasing its effectiveness. Brain temperatures are usually controlled to a greater extent than general body temperatures, they are subject to less fluctuation and are controlled by sophisticated mechanisms.

As water economy is as important in deserts as temperature control, it ia necessary to consider a number of questions in discussing thermal balance (Taylor 1970a):

- How much water do animals lose by evaporation when that resource is available ad libitum?;
- Is evaporation reduced when water is in short supply?;
- Is evaporation increased as ambient temperature rises?; and
- Does variable body temperature (bradymetaboly) play a role in reducing evaporation?

Coupled, of necessity, with these physiological processes are adaptations of morphology and behaviour which might assist in maintaining the body temperature in the thermoneutral zone of each species.

3.2 Bradymetaboly in the Dromedary

The normal temperature variation in a fully hydrated camel does not exceed a diurnal range of about 2° C and is in the range of about 36° C to 38° C. In

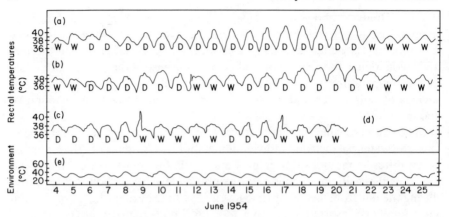

Fig. 3.3. Temperature relations in hydrated and dehydrated camels and donkeys and in man (Schmidt-Nielsen et al. 1957 b)

a 500kg animal the heat stored as a result of a diurnal variation in temperature of 2° C would be of the order of 4.2 x 10^6J. In dehydrated camels, when considerations of energy and water conservation become more important, temperature variation can be as much as 8° C in the range of 34° C to 42° C but a more normal range is of about 6° C from 35° C to 41° C. These extremes are outside the range of comfort of most mammals and would be lethal for many. As can be seen from Fig. 3.3, there is a much wider variation in the camel than in the donkey and in man. A temperature range of 6° C in a 500 kg camel enables 1.26 x 10^7J of energy to be stored, equivalent to the conservation of about 6 litres of water if sweat had to be used to dissipate the same amount.

The reduced temperature gradient between the camel and its immediate environment resulting from an elevated body temperature assists further in reducing heat gain, as the gain is proportional to the gradient. Energy gained during the heat of the day is dissipated to the environment when ambient temperatures are cooler at night. The combined strategies of an elevated body temperature leading to a shallow gradient during the day and heat loss at night allow water loss required to maintain a temperature within the acceptable range for the camel to be reduced from 4.7% to 1.4% of the body water pool (Schmidt-Nielsen 1964).

The metabolic rate of fully hydrated camels increases in the normal way as body temperature rises and the metabolic rate decreases as the body temperature falls (Schmidt-Nielsen et al. 1967). The Q^{10} is slightly over two in this state. An increased metabolic rate adds substantially to the heat load but, as water is available, the additional heat generated can be dissipated without problem through evaporative cooling. Endogenous heat is both a by-product and an end product of metabolism and, in zebu cattle not under stress, may constitute almost one-third of the total heat load on an animal (Finch 1976). The upper critical heat load may be exceeded due to the oxygen cost of evaporative cooling if metabolism at high ambient temperatures continues to increase (Robertshaw and Finch 1976).

It has been shown in the fully watered camel that thyroid activity is higher in the summer, when temperatures are higher, than in the winter (Yagil, Etzion and Ganani 1978). There is also an increase in activity of the thyroid-stimulating hormone-releasing factor (TSH) and of thyroxine (T4). When dehydrated, the activity of TSH continued unchanged but T4 secretion was reduced, as was that of triiodothyroxine (T3). It was considered that, as food consumption was not diminished in dehydrated camels, the reduction in thyroid activity was associated with reduced water and that the decline in activity was important to the dehydrated camel because the generation of metabolic heat was lessened and respiratory water losses were reduced. Depressed thyroid function could allow greater fluctuations in temperature and TSH concentrations would remain the same, as the reduction in T4 causes a reflex secretion of the TSH and degradation of TSH in the kidneys is reduced through the diminished renal blood flow (Yagil and Berlyne 1978a). It should be noted that in other animals chronic exposure to heat results in depressed thyroid activity as well as in reduced plasma cortisol and growth hormone concentrations and turnover rates. All three hormones are calorigenic and act in cooperation (Thompson 1976) so the net result of habituation to heat is some reduction in metabolic rate.

In desert-adapted mammals subject to an intense radiant environment, theoretical considerations would lead one to conclude that they should possess smooth reflective coats and a black skin. Additional advantages would accrue to water conservation if the pelage were not so thick as to prevent evaporation at the skin surface but not so thin as to allow too much heat to reach the body surface. A light-coloured coat results in high albedo values and a black skin absorba most of the ultra violet light, thus preventing damage to body tissues. A camel in its natural summer coat has hair that is about 30mm long on its flanks and 15mm to 20mm long on the belly and legs. With a coat of this type a camel is able to maintain a lower body temperature than a shorn camel. A camel in its natural summer coat therefore requires to expend less energy in heat dissipation than a shorn camel.

In the colder areas of deserts (Mediterranean Sahara and Australia) camels grow longer coats in winter. Camels in winter coats may have a temperature of 65° C at the surface, while in the shorter, sleeker and shinier coat of summer, temperatures at the hair/air interface do not exceed 46° C (Macfarlane 1977).

At very high temperatures and constant heat loads even camels need to dissipate heat. Many mammals achieve evaporative cooling through an increased respiratory rate rather than by sweating from the body or coat surface. Respiratory cooling is relatively more expensive in water than is sweating as faster respiration rates require more energy to be used. Normal respiratory rates in camels are in the range of 6 to 11 breaths/min (average = 8) in the Sahara and range from 10 to 12 in Australia. Under heat stress, respiration rates increase to levels of 8 to 18 (average = 16) in the Sahara and to 20 to 24/min in Australia (Schmidt-Nielsen 1964; Macfarlane 1968). There appears to be no logical explanation why respiration rates differ, nor is it possible, as the experiments were done at different places at different times, to say whether the differences are significant. Such low respiration rates do not result in significantly increased evaporation. Respiration rates increase very markedly in many other ruminants and in the dog may be as high as 400min. At such rapid rates water loss and energy expenditure are both very high.

Camels avoid energy expenditure, when they need to use water for cooling, by sweating. They do not sweat continuously as do many other mammals (Macfarlane 1964) and sweat evaporates directly from the skin. The latent heat of evaporation is therefore taken from the skin rather than from the surface of the pelage. Early reports that the camel did not sweat (e.g. Leonard 1894) were probably due to sweat evaporating at the surface. These early reports also led to the conclusion that camels did not have sweat glands (Dowling and Nay 1962).

The camel dermis is thicker than that of cattle and sheep and it has been demonstrated that camels do, in fact, have sweat glands which are deeply embedded in the skin (Lee and Schmidt-Nielsen 1962). Camels have an epidermal thickness of about 0.6mm and a dermis which is about 3.0mm deep. There are an average of 200 sweat glands per square centimetre on camels, about one-quarter of the number found on cattle. Structural changes have shown that they are more active in hot summer temperatures than in winter ones in Israel (Sekles et al. 1979). The sweat glands of camels do not appear to be innervated and in this respect they are similar to those of other domestic ruminants. The nerve supply to the skin itself is also similar to that found in other domestic animals (Rollinson, Injidi and Jenkinson 1972). A prominent feature of the camel's skin is the deeply pigmented dendritic cells in the epidermis and upper part of the hair follicle. These cells contain choline-sterase and may, together with the nature of the coat, provide an efficient barrier to solar radiation.

Camel sweat contains about four times as many potassium ions (40.1mEq/litre) as sodium ones (9.5mEq/litre) and also contains relatively large amounts of bicarbonate (HCO_3-) ions. The pH is 8.2 to 8.5 (Macfarlane, Morris and Howard 1963). Sweating is controlled by aldosterone and vasopressin, also known as the anti-diuretic hormone (ADH) and, as thermoregulation has preference over homeostasis, the relative amounts of secretion of these hormones account for the hypotonicity of camel sweat to blood and for the low sodium content (Yagil 1985).

The camel has a number of non-physiological mechanisms for reducing the radiant heat load and its absorption. Morphological adaptations include the overall size, the long legs and neck, and the hump. As almost all fat is stored in the hump, heat can be dissipated more freely over the rest of the body surface. A direct relationship exists between blood flow and heat loss. Heat loss is proportional to blood flow as long as the difference between deep body and surface temperature remains constant (Thauer 1965). Blood flow is greater in the peripheral parts of an animal than it is in the central body, and the long legs of the camel can therefore be seen as conferring considerable benefit in heat dissipation.

In general, the camel is unable to escape from direct radiation. It therefore attempts to minimise its effects. It does this by a wide variety of methods. When radiation is high, a camel will attempt to be as inactive as possible during the day. It couches early in the morning before the ground has had time to become hot and its slight elevation from the ground, due to the way it settles and to the dispositon of its body and leg pads, enables air to circulate freely and convectional heat transfer to take place. Groups of camels huddle together, thus reducing the total surface area presented to the incoming radiation. Camels will preferentially browse at night or in the early morning or late evening when temperatures are cooler. If forced to graze during the heat of the day, camels restrict movement as much as possible and almost invariably graze towards or away from the most intense heat source, the sun, in order to minimise absorption. Couched camels also adopt the same tactic, moving their position to follow the sun throughout the day.

As already noted, the endogenous heat of metabolism can account for as much as 30% of the total heat load on an animal (Finch 1976). Camels do not lose appetite to the same extent as other species under heat stress and dehydration. Reductions in feed intake and feeding activities – which may account for as much as 90 per cent of day-time activity of wild and domestic ruminants (Lewis 1977, 1978) – could, however, lead to a reduction of total heat load of from 10 to 20%.

3.3 Domesticated Small Ruminants

Small ruminants are apparently less well adapted to desesrt life than the dromedary. Homeothermy is much more strictly enforced in goats and sheep than in camels. Neither goats nor sheep apparently exhibit large changes in temperature.

Native African hair sheep and goats can store only small amounts of heat within their normal temperature range of 36° C to 38° C (Maloiy and Taylor 1971). At higher ambient temperatures both species resort to panting as a means of evaporative cooling and it has been assumed that heat tolerance is only possible in these species when sufficient water is available for it to be used to facilitate evaporative cooling (Quartermain 1964; Bligh 1972). Some sheep types in the Middle East have higher body temperatures in the range of 38.7° C to 40.5° C and thus may be better adapted to desert conditions (Degen 1977c).

3.3.1 Sheep

Desert-adapted sheep often have fat deposited in one area of the body in a manner analogous to the hump of the camel. The extreme case is exhibited by African fat-rumped sheep, notably the Blackhead Persian which is now widespread in southern Africa but was developed in the deserts of the Horn of Africa. In this type (Fig. 3.4) almost all fat is deposited high on the rump (the tail is very short and protrudes from this grotesque mass like a small finger) although there are also fat pads behind the poll and some kidney fat is deposited. The coat is white and of short, sleek hair and reflects the short-wave radiation very efficiently. Only the head is black.

The Blackhead Persian adopts the same grazing orizntation as the camel and is almost always oriented with its long axis towards the sun. It has been shown in southern Africa that the heat load in sheep aligned perpendicularly to the sun is reduced to approximately half of that in horizontally oriented animals –183 W against 374 W at a sun elevation of 8° and 203 W against 381 W at a sun elevation of 42° (Hofmeyr and Louw 1987). Other types of desert sheep with fat tails (as opposed to fat rumps) are widespread throughout the arid zones of east and north-east Africa, Mediterranean Africa and the Middle East countries. Yet other sheep have relatively long legs and some have extremely long and broad ears, which presumably assist in heat dissipation.

Fig. 3.4. Ectopic fat deposition in a desert-adapted sheep, the Blackhead Persian

Many breeds of sheep have been artificially selected by man for high wool production. The apparent paradox of the world's best-known wool-producing breed, the Merino, providing its best performance in the arid areas of Australia, South Africa and South America therefore needs some explanation. The outer fleece temperature can be as high as 85° C, resulting in a reversed temperature gradient from the animal to the environment. The temperature at the body surface under the thick cover of wool does not exceed 40° C. The wool therefore acts as an efficient insulator by intercepting much of the short wave radiation and scattering long wave radiation. Australian Merino sheep shorn in summer had a water turnover rate double that of sheep in full wool (Macfarlane, Howard and Morris 1966). At night the wool preserves the body temperature by preventing the dissipation of heat from the surface zone. It has, however, been pointed out that wool has some advantages in hot dry climates, but the reverse is the case in hot humid ones (McDowell 1972).

Sheep respond to heat load by sweating and panting. Their sweating mechanism is not, however, very efficient and the magnitude of the response to heat declines over time (Robertshaw 1968). This inability of sheep to maintain a high rate of sweating has resulted in their principal cooling strategy being that of panting or respiratory heat loss. Under heat load the panting rate of sheep increases by 674% (Hales and Webster 1967). Sheep under heat stress therefore need constant access to water unless they can adjust their behaviour sufficiently to overcome their lack of physiological adaptation.

3.3.2 Goats

Goats in deserts have physiological and morphological adaptations similar to sheep, with the exception of fat deposition. Goats lay down little fat under normal nutritional conditions. When they are in exceptional condition as a result of good feed supplies, the small amount of fat they do store is mostly in the viscera and around the kidneys. Long legs and exceptionally long and broad ears are seen in many desert goat types (Fig. 3.5). Most goats have thin, supple skins and short, fine hair and many desert breeds are light-coloured. There is some evidence, at least in Africa, that pastoral tribes are aware of the advantages of light coat colours and actively select for them. In one study of cattle in Kenya (Finch and Western 1977), a linear relationship ($y = 0.07x - 73.9$ where y was the percentage of light-coloured animals and x the potential evapotranspiration, which in this case was used as a proxy for heat stress) was demonstrated between the proportion of light-coloured animals and the level of environmental stress.

There are, nonetheless, many types of goats in the arid zones which are dark in colour. One is the Red Sokoto of northern Nigeria and southern Niger. The most widely known anachronistic goat in this respect is the black Bedouin breed of the Negev and Sinai deserts in the Middle East. Attention

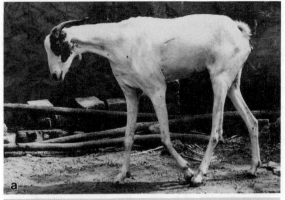

Fig. 3.5. Long legs and long and broad ears in West African Sahel and Sudanese Nubian goats adapted to dersert conditions

to the apparent anomaly of a black goat in a desert environment was first brought to scientific attention some 20 years ago (Shkolnik, Borut and Choshniak 1972). Since that time much has been written about it (Finch et al. 1980), although most published work relates to water economy rather than, strictly speaking, to temperature regulation (Choshniak and Shkolnik 1977, 1978; Choshniak et al. 1984; Shkolnik and Choshniak 1984; Choshniak, Wittenberg and Saham 1987). Once again theoretical considerations would lead to the conclusion that the black colour would be a disadvantage in an intense radiant environment. As black goats are the commonest domestic animal in the Negev and Sinai deserts (they are also common in many other desert areas, including Syria, Lebanon, Tunisia, Morocco and Sudan), the possibility was considered that the black coat might be an adaptation to the desert environment.

Experiments were undertaken on black goats, a white goat from the same environment and a female ibex (*Capra ibex*): the ibex is basically fawn in colour. The results of the study showed that on full exposure to the sun the net heat gain of black goats was considerably greater than that of both the white goat and the ibex (Table 3.1). There were no differences in metabolic

Table 3.1. A comparison of heat gain (W/m^2) of black and white goats and ibex under exposed and shaded conditions (adapted from Finch et al. 1980)

	Heat gain	=	Heat evaporated	+	Heat storage	−	Metabolic heat
Exposed to sun							
Black goat	104		177		8		81
White goat	49		123		7		81
Ibex	62		134		10		82
Shaded							
Black goat	24		92		10		78
White goat	15		89		8		82
Ibex	18		79		17		78

heat production or heat storage among the three types of animal and all the additional heat gained by the black goats was lost through evaporation. There were no differences in heat balance when all animals were confined in the shade. The difference in heat gain in sunlight was due almost entirely to short wave (0.3–2.5m) absorption, this being almost twice as much in black goats (288 W/m^2) when compared to white goats (153 W/m^2) or ibex (158 W/m^2). Long wave radiation (2.5m) was absorbed in very similar amounts (– 460 W/m2) by all three groups.

Black goats do not therefore have a comparative advantage in thermoregulation at hot temperatures. It is then suggested that there are advantages to these goats in the winter, when they warm up earlier and more quickly than light-coloured goats. Similar advantages, leading to lower death rates following drought and starvation, have been postulated for black over white cattle in Kenya (Finch and Western 1977). It has, however, been rather surprisingly shown that under the black burnous worn by Bedouin the temperature does not differ from that under white robes, in spite of much higher outer garment temperatures (Shkolnik et al. 1980).

In another study of black goats in India in the winter (Goyal and Ghosh 1987) albedo measurements showed an absorption of about 82% of the incident radiation which was calculated at from 656 to 815 W/m^2 for four goats. This value is similar to the one found for Sinai goats, but in India heat gains were only 30 to 56W/m^2 or about 6.3% of the heat falling on a horizontal surface. It was concluded that in black goats most of the incoming heat was re-radiated at or near the surface of the coat as long wave radiation. This hypothesis is also supported by other workers (Hutchinson, Allen and Spence 1975; Cena and Monteith 1975; Walsberg, Campbell and King 1978).

An additional adaptation to hot environments shown by both goats and sheep relates to the scrotum. In both species the testicles are often enclosed in a long and pendulous sac. Semen quantity and quality is better in animals in which a further refinement, the splitting of the scrotal sac into two separate

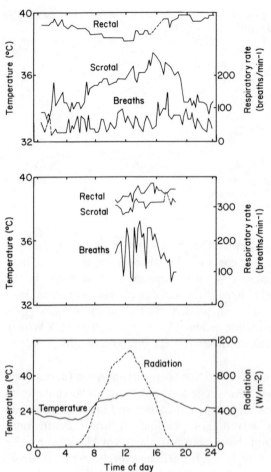

Fig. 3.6. Rectal and subcutaneous scrotal temperatures and respiration rates of free ranging and restrained Merino rams in New South Wales (adpated from Brown 1974)

halves for more than one third of its length, is present. Testes temperatures can be further reduced as a result of coiling the arteries around the scrotal veins (Waites and Moule 1961).

Behavioural adaptations are also important in maintaining a low scrotal temperature (Brown 1974). Merino sheep in an open paddock that were able to rest in shade during the day were able to maintain scrotal temperatures, as well as respiration rates, much below those of animals which were forced to spend the hottest part of the day in the open (Fig. 3.6).

The horns of goats may also have a thermoregulatory function, this being the only superficial area with a major drainage of blood through the cavernous sinus (Taylor 1966).

3.4   Wild Ruminants

Most wild ruminants are too large to retreat from the desert environment at the most stressful time of the day. The plethora of species has adapted a multiplicity of characteristics in order to overcome the problems posed by high heat loads. The relative importance of each strategy or tactic is species-specific. Heat gain and loss are more rapid in small than in large species. Body temperature is maintained in the thermal neutral zone by evaporative cooling or is allowed to rise heterothermically. If evaporative cooling is employed, the relative importance of respiratory or cutaneous evaporation varies. Dehydration is responsible for different methods of temperature regulation. Depth, density and colour of the coat affect the reflectivity and absorption of heat.

As for camels and domestic ruminants the two main strategies of temperature regulation in non-domestic ruminants are bradymetaboly and evaporative cooling (Taylor 1970a, b).

3.4.1   Oryx and Eland

Both oryx (*Oryx beisa*) and eland (*Taurotragus oryx*) exhibit a considerable degree of bradymetaboly. The Beisa and fringe-eared oryx (these are two very similar sub-species) live in the very arid regions of East Africa from northern Tanzania to central Ethiopia. When dehydrated, they are able to allow their body temperatures to rise to such an extent that it is usually higher than the ambient (Taylor 1969a). The difference between the two temperatures is maintained so that animals can lose both metabolic and radiant heat by conduction and radiation without having to resort to evaporative cooling until very high ambient and body temperatures (41° C) are achieved. Although the oryx sweats when hydrated, it does not do so when dehydrated, but pants instead. Experiments have shown that sweating in the oryx is controlled by adrenalin, but adrenalin flow is blocked by the nervous system in the dehydrated state. When fully hydrated, the oryx temperature fluctuated from 35.7° C to 42.1° C. In a laboratory situation oryx were able to withstand a temperature of 45° C for at least 8 hours when dehydrated, without any damage to body tissues resulting. No experiments of this nature have been carried out on oryx in the wild, but unlike eland, with which they are sympatric, they do not seek shade in the hottest part of the day. Because of this behavioural difference it has been suggested that oryx would be more suitable as domestic animals than eland (Lewis 1978), although most domestication attempts, for example in South Africa and in Russia, have concentrated on the eland. It was suggested (Lewis 1977) that the better tolerance of oryx to heat stress was in part due to differences in coat characteristics. Of four species under study (buffalo, *Syncerus caffer*, and zebu cattle in addition to

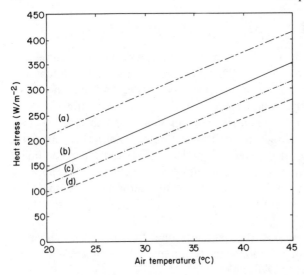

Fig. 3.7. Predicted relationship between heat stress and air temperature in ruminants with different coat characteristics: *(a)* buffalo; *(b)* eland; *(c)* zebu cattle; *(d)* oryx (Lewis 1977)

oryx and eland), the oryx was subject to least stress (Fig. 3.7), mainly because the coat has an absorption coefficient of 0.65 and a structure which is dense with relatively long hairs at 0.4mm. Zebu cattle (absorption coefficient 0.78, coat length 0.3mm) suffered less stress than eland (absorption coefficient 0.75, coat length 0.2mm) and buffalo suffered most of all with a black, very sparse coat. The ability to support very high temperatures without resorting to evaporative cooling is a major strategy of the oryx which, in the wild, must frequently survive for very long periods without access to water. The fine and light-coloured coat of the oryx also reflects much of the radiant environment. Although they have not been studied in detail, it seems probable that two other closely related species of oryx, the gemsbok in the Kalahari and Namib deserts of southern Africa, and the scimitar-horned oryx (*Oryx dammah*) in the Sahara, have similar attributes.

The oryx is a medium-sized ungulate whose body mass prevents too rapid heating during the day. The eland is a larger antelope and, although it does not penetrate as far into the desert as does the oryx, it is also subject to very high ambient temperatures. In the laboratory, an eland in water balance varied its body temperature from 33.9° C to 41.2° C (Taylor 1969b). The increase in body temperature is slow, due to the large size of the animal, and under natural conditions it is unlikely that the highest body temperature is achieved until the ambient temperature is on the decrease. Heterothermy is reinforced by the behaviour of the eland which, in its natural savanna environment, seeks shade during the hottest part of the day. It is thus able to retreat from the worst effects of heat. In contrast to the hartebeest (*Alcelaphus buselaphus*), the surface temperature of the eland is always less than the deep body temperature (Finch 1972a) and heat therefore flows

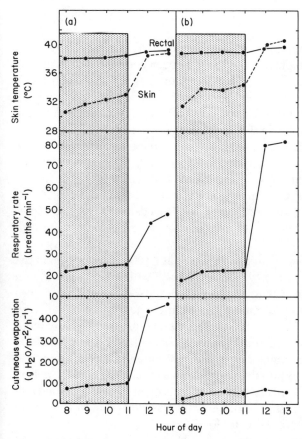

Fig. 3.8. Effect of environmental conditions on skin and rectal temperature, respiration and cutaneous evaporation in (a) eland and (b) hartebeest (Finch 1972 a)

outwards. Sweating in the eland begins at an ambient temperature of 32° C to 34° C, but only small volumes of water are lost. At 38° C to 40° C sweating increases to four or five times more than the low initial level – 400 to 500gH_2O/ m^2/h. Eland also increase their respiration rate at high temperatures, but this method is much less used in this species than in the hartebeest (Fig. 3.8).

The coat of the eland is relatively sparse and reddish brown in colour and it absorbs 71 to 79% of solar radiation. The hartebeest absorbs less than this, 60 to 67%, probably because its coat is lighter in colour, is thick and dense and each hair is tipped with white. However, the combined reflectance and conductance of the fur in both species are an important barrier, preventing much of the heat from reaching the body surface.

In dehydrated oryx the metabolic rate is reduced by as much as 30% at night and that of the eland by 5%. At these lower metabolic rates deeper breathing enables greater amounts of oxygen to be extracted from the inhaled air and less heat is lost with the exhaled air.

3.4.2   Springbok

The springbok is a small antelope of the southern African semi-desert areas, particularly of the Karoo biome. It has for long been considered to be a well-adapted arid zone dweller and to be independent of free water when this is not available. In an experiment recently carried out on a restrained springbok (Hofmeyr and Louw 1987), the effects of ambient temperature, solar radiation and windspeed were studied. The springbok does not appear to be a bradyme-tabolic animal. It responds to heat stress by attempting to maintain its core body temperature within the range of 38.6° C to 40.5° C. In this restrained animal, behavioural regulation was not possible and temperatures at the fur surface were as high as 54° C at an ambient temperature of 28° C and 60° C at an ambient temperature of 34° C when windspeeds were less than 2m/s. Windspeeds greater than 2m/s led to a large drop of 15° C to 25° C in coat surface temperature.

Respiratory cooling appears to be the main path of heat dissipation in the springbok. A linear relationship (y = 6.3 x – 104.7 with y being respiration rate and x being fur surface temperature) was established between pelage temperature and number of respirations per minute. The respiration rate rose from 40/min at 22° C to 275/min at 60° C. Peripheral sensors of heat are more important than deep body temperature in heat control, as shown by a better correlation between pelage temperature and respiration rate. The springbok reacts very rapidly to thermal stress by respiratory cooling and at pelage temperatures of over 50° C pants with its mouth open. Sweating is also an important source of heat loss and can be as high as $79gH_2O/m^2/h$ ($53 W/m^2$) in an ambient temperature of 25° C to 30° C.

At night when temperatures were low, and perhaps exacerbated by the wind chill factor, springbok were observed to shiver. Fur surface temperatures were as much as 8° C higher than ambient at night and infrared thermometry indicated that the fur is a poor insulator.

In the springbok experiment, ear and horn temperatures were also measured. Both of these generally followed changes in the ambient temperature, but in response to changes in radiation (sun behind cloud or appearing from behind cloud) vasoconstriction or vasodilation resulted in very rapid changes in ear temperature (Fig. 3.9). When springbok were subjected to intense heat loads during the day, ear temperatures remained well in excess of body temperature for long periods. This clearly demonstrates the role of the ears in heat balance and could account for the very large ears of some sheep and goats, as already noted (Sect. 3.3.2, Fig. 3.5). The value of large ears as an aid to cooling has been contested, as even enormous ears have an area equivalent to less than 2% of the total body surface (McDowell 1972). On the other hand, the capacity of the vascular bed and the blood flow can be greatly increased by vasodilation and by arterio-venous anastomoses (Goodall 1955). Peripheral vasodilation is of overall importance

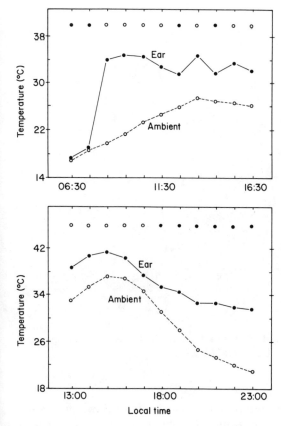

Fig. 3.9. Ambient temperature and ear temperature of a restrained springbok at different times of day and under different solar conditions (Hofmeyr and Louw 1987)

in improving heat flow to the surface to facilitate evaporative, radiative and convective loss of heat (Thompson 1976). To be at its most efficient, this method relies on temperature differences between the animal and the immediate environment. Peripheral vasodilation is therefore more effective at night, this probably being the reason that the elephant (*Loxodonta africana*), which has a temperature lability of 6° C (Elder and Rodgers 1975), and which uses its huge ears as an aid to cooling, only increases blood flow and vasodilation at night (Hiley 1975).

In addition to physiological responses, springbok exhibit a marked behavioural response to heat stress. At ambient temperatures varying from 16° C to 38° C and at total radiation levels of 1000 W/m² animals maintained deep body temperatures in the range 37.5° C to 41.0° C whether hydrated or dehydrated. Highest body temperatures occurred, as expected, between 14:00 h and 16:00 h. The unrestrained springbok did not show the same thermal stress as the restrained animal, and open-mouthed panting and extremely high respiration rates were not noted. This was because animals sought shade when it was available.

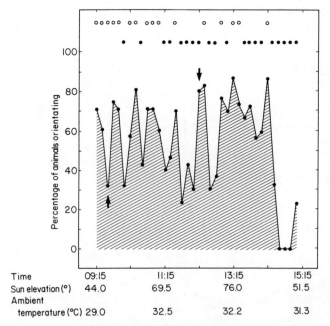

Fig. 3.10. Behavioural orientation of Springbok towards the sun (arrows indicate herd moving as are unit) (Hofmeyr and Louw 1987)

Of equal or possibly greater importance than shading behaviour was the orientation of the body in relation to the sun. On clear sunny days 61% of animals aligned the long axis of their bodies to the sun, but on intermittent sunny and rainy days only 32% of animals adopted this posture (Fig. 3.10). The usual advantages of reduced area exposed to the direct solar radiation accrue from this behaviour, the difference in solar heat load being 101 W/m2 at a sun elevation of 16°, this being reduced to 6 W/m^2 at 79°. The overall difference in the two orientation patterns was a 62% reduction in the heat load in the course of a day. By orienting perpendicular to the sun, springbok also benefit from the high reflectivity of their white rumps (0.72) or their faces. As there is more white on the rump than on the face, especially when animals are grazing head down, animals preferred to graze away from, rather than towards, the sun.

3.4.3 Dorcas Gazelle

The Dorcas gazelle (*Gazella dorcas*) is the ecological equivalent, in the northern African southern Saharan zone, of the springbok in the Kalahari and the Namib. As with the springbok, the Dorcas is not bradymetabolic and it begins to sweat at an ambient temperature of 22° C and a body temperature of 38° C. The main sources of heat dissipation are thermal panting and sweating (Ghobrial 1970a, 1974). In the cool season the gazelle (which weighs about 16kg) has a requirement of 590g water per day and uses about 160g of this in temperature control. All of this water can be obtained in the food. In the hot season the water requirement increases to 840g per day as a result of higher temperatures and a greater need for evaporative cooling. Much of the food requirement is obtained from the relatively succulent thorny acacia *A. tortilis* (Ghobrial 1970a). In the hot season the Dorcas gazelle does have need of free water, probably at least in part because appetite is depressed with heat.

Some protection from heat is also obtained via the pelage. The coat consists of a short, dense undercoat with a covering of guard hairs up to 35mm long (Ghobrial 1970b). The coat can be piloerected to form an insulating barrier, and it is also suggested that it may hold a layer of humid air which prevents excessive water loss through the sweat glands and the skin.

It appears, however, and rather surprisingly, that the Dorcas gazelle is not very well adapted to life in extremely arid deserts and has to resort to mechanisms of escape (seasonal migration to food sources and/or cooler areas such as the Red Sea hills in Sudan) and retreat (shade-seeking at midday) to survive.

3.4.4   Grant's Gazelle and Thomson's Gazelle

The morphological characteristics of both these small gazelles are very similar, although Grant's gazelle (*Gazella granti*) has a mature body size (25kg in females and 40kg in males) about twice as heavy as Thomson's gazelle (*G. thomsoni*, 13kg in females and 20–25kg in males). The species are sympatric over much of their range in northern Tanzania and southern and central Kenya. Where both species occur together they often run in mixed herds. Grant's gazelle has a wider distribution compared with Thomson's, extending south to central Tanzania and northwards through northern Kenya into Ethiopia and Somalia. The range extension of Grant's gazelle is into arid and very arid areas where Thomson's gazelle does not appear to be able to penetrate.

In a simulated desert environment (12 hours at 22° C and 12 hours at 40° C), fully hydrated gazelle of both species adopted respiratory cooling as their main mode of temperature control (Taylor 1972). Grant's lost 83% of total body water through evaporation and Thomson's 82% when both species were fully watered. At ambient air temperatures of 22° C the respiratory rate of both species was about 15/min , but this increased to about 200 (and even up to 300) respirations/min at 40° C. Both Grant's and Thomson's panted with closed mouths. Gazelles have functional sweat glands (Robertshaw and Taylor

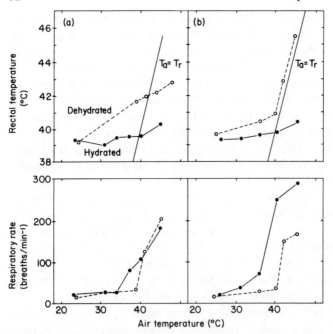

Fig. 3.11. Physiological parameters of *(a)* Thomson's and *(b)* Grant's gazelles under free and restricted water regimes in a simulated desert environment (Taylor 1972)

1969) but cutaneous water loss accounts for only a small proportion of evaporative losses. This is partly explained by the fact that, although the frequency of release of sweat from glands increases with increasing heat, the rate of water loss between periods of activity is greatly reduced.

In dehydrated gazelle under the same experimental regime evaporative water losses accounted for 63% of total water in Grant's gazelle but only 31% in Thomson's. Under restricted water conditions, therefore, both species reduced evaporative cooling, mainly by keeping their respiration rate low and by resorting to bradymetaboly (Fig. 3.11). In both species, body temperature exceeded the ambient during the hot period (41.6° C in Thomson's and 41.0° C in Grant's) and dropped to normal levels in the cool period. The build up in body temperature in these small mammals is much more rapid, as might be expected from a lack of thermal inertia due to their smaller size, than in the larger oryx or eland.

It has been considered paradoxical that under these conditions the more mesic Thomson's gazelle should apparently have a more efficient water conservation mechanism than the more xeric Grant's gazelle (Taylor 1972). When temperatures were raised in excess of the 40° C simulated desert normally used in this series of experiments, the Thomson's gazelle was unable to raise its body temperature sufficiently to maintain it higher than the ambient even when dehydrated. The respiratory rate of Thomson's at these very high temperatures increased to allow evaporative cooling to become the main mode of temperature control. Conversely, even at very high temperatures, dehydrated Grant's continued to elevate their temperatures in excess of the ambient and rectal temperatures as high as 45° C to 46° C were recorded. The respiratory rate of Grant's increased concurrently with body temperature but to a much lesser extent than Thomson's. It seems, then, that Grant's gazelle would be better adapted to the short periods of very intense solar radiation and heat, which are common around midday in deserts, than the smaller species. This ability to support short intense periods of radiation might account for the range extension of Grant's in comparison to Thomson's gazelle.

Behavioural mechanisms have not been reported in either species in an effort to escape or retreat from heat. Neither species systematically seeks shade. Some slight additional advantage to Grant's might occur as it has a paler-coloured coat than Thomson's (and the adult male Grant's does not have the dark flank stripes) and therefore probably has superior short wave reflectance.

3.4.5 Dik-dik

Two species of dik-dik are found in the semi-arid to arid areas (Kirk's dik-dik, *Madoqua kirki*) and in the arid to extremely arid areas (Guenther's dik-dik, *M. guentheri*) of Africa. Dik-dik have a disjunct distribution from southern Africa through central Tanzania to Ethiopia and Somalia. There is one report of dik-dik presence in Jebel Marra in Darfur Province of Sudan (Cloudsley-Thompson 1965) but earlier (Thomas and Hinton 1923) and later (Wilson 1979) comprehensive surveys did not find it there. As they are almost exclusively browsers dik-dik tend to be more numerous in spiny *Acacia* areas and *Commiphora* thicket. They are extremely small antelopes, mature weights being in the range of 2kg to 8kg.

The dik-dik is a partially bradymetabolic mammal, being able to elevate its body temperature when dehydrated (Schoen 1972; Maloiy 1973a; Hoppe 1977). Under experimental conditions at air tempeature of 20° C to 45° C rectal temperature remained higher than ambient temperature when the latter did not exceed 40° C. When fully hydrated, body temperature increased relatively slowly but in dehydrated animals body temperatures increased rapidly at ambient temperatures above 35° C. Hydrated animals did not allow body temperature to exceed 41° C at 45° C ambient but dehydrated animals had body temperatures in excess of 43° C (Fig. 3.12).

The main method of reducing body temperature is by evaporative cooling. The dik-dik seems to conform to the small antelope model in terms of evaporative cooling and uses the respiratory route preferentially over the cutaneous one. Respiration rates increased from about 25/min at 20° C to

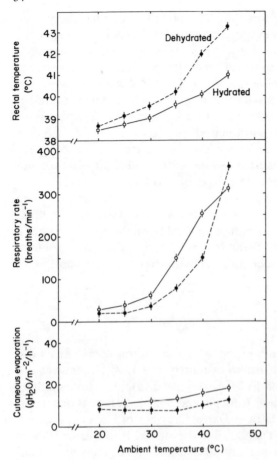

Fig. 3.12. Rectal temperatures, respiration rates and cutaneous evaporation of hydrated and dehydrated dik-dik at temperatures from 20°C to 45°C (Maloiy 1973a)

about 250/min at 40° C in hydrated animals: hydrated animals at 45° C ambient temperature breathed at about 300 respirations/min. In dehydrated dik-dik, respirations were about 150/min at 40° C but this temperature appears to be a threshold and there was a very rapid increase to about 370/min in dehydrated dik-dik at 45° C. Open-mouth panting was resorted to at the faster rates.

Sweating rates were low in both treatments and were slightly higher in fully watered animals than in dehydrated one throughout the temperature range from 20° C to 45° C. A low density of sweat glands of about 190/cm² on the body surface must explain to some extent the low cutaneous evaporative rate. Sweating rates were 19gH₂O/m²/h on the rib cage where the sample was taken but, over the whole body surface, probably range from 3gH₂0/m²/h to 6gH₂O/m²/h. Sweating rates could be induced to increase following injections of adrenalin and noradrenalin, showing that the mechanism, like that of other Bovidae, is under adrenergic-neurone control (Robertshaw and Taylor 1969).

Behavioural mechanisms used by the did-dik to reduce heat load include crepuscular and nocturnal feeding with reduced to minimal activity during the hot part of the day (Tinley 1969; pers. observ.).

3.4.6   Other Species

None of hartebeest (*Alcelaphus* spp.), wildebeest (*Connochaetes* spp.), buffalo or waterbuck (*Kobus* spp.) exhibits bradymetaboly (Taylor, Robertshaw and Hofmann 1969; Taylor, Spinage and Lyman 1969; Taylor 1970b; Finch 1972a, b). All of these species can live either in or close to desert areas, but the buffalo, and in particular the waterbuck (as its name suggests), are more or less dependent on a favourable micro-habitat within the arid zones. Waterbuck, for example, are never found more than 2km from permanent water and prefer to remain in "islands" of woodland and thicket as is the case in Tarangire in northern Tanzania (Lamprey 1963) and Awash in Ethiopia (pers. observ.). Buffalo have very similar requirements. Both species are grazers rather than browsers and the preferred location is not related to food availability. Hartebeest and wildebeest, also grazers, are found in open grassland areas, farther away from water, but having recourse to the same source as waterbuck and buffalo in both Tarangire and on the Masai steppe (Lamprey 1964).

Hartebeest maintain a constant body temperature of 38° C to 40° C in either sun or shade, the main means of thermoregulation being by panting. At high ambient temperatures, panting rates increase fourfold and may reach 200 breaths/min. Losses through sweating are comparatively low, with respiratory losses accounting for 62% of total evaporative water loss. The effects of radiant heat are reduced by the light-coloured and dense coat. Absorption of heat is fairly low (0.58) and about 80% of this is re-radiated as the coat surface rises to 46° C. The control mechanism initiating evaporative loss appears to be the skin temperature. Hartebeest start to pant at skin temperatures of 36° C and pant with the mouth open at high temperatures (Maloiy and Hopcraft 1971; Finch 1972a, b).

Wildebeest have a narrower range of body temperature than hartebeest, in the range of 39° C to 40° C. The principal control mechanism is the respiratory route. Cutaneous water loss is small although there are functional sweat glands. Respiratory rate increases in a manner similar to that of the hartebeest and panting starts at an ambient temperature of 28° C. Panting in the wildebeest presumably is advantageous because it will allow the skin temperature to exceed the body temperature. Less blood therefore requires to be pumped to the surface and heat gained from the environment will be less than if skin temperature was maintained at a lower level. A low environmental heat load could more than offset the metabolic heat resulting from panting (Robertshaw and Taylor 1969; Taylor, Robertshaw and Hofmann 1969; Taylor 1970a).

Buffalo maintain their body temperature at 38° C to 40° C but they rely on the cutaneous route of evaporation rather than on the respiratory one. Sweating rates of $50gH_2O/m^2/h$ at an ambient temperature of 20° C increase to 250 $gH_2O/m^2/h$ at 40° C. When dehydrated, buffalo sweat less than when fully watered and they pant at high temperatures although the water lost via the respiratory tract is small (Taylor 1970a, b).

Waterbuck appear to be intermediate between the hartebeest and the wildbeest on the one hand and the buffalo on the other hand in terms of evaporative cooling. The normal body temperature is within the range of 38° C to 41° C. At low ambient temperatures evaporative losses are slightly higher via the respiratory route than via the cutaneous one. The situation is reversed at high temperatures, and under experimental conditions hydrated waterbuck at 40° C lose more than twice as much water through sweating as through the respiratory tract. When dehydrated at 40° C, waterbuck lose as much as 12% of their body weight in 12 hours in an attempt to maintain body temperature in the thermoneutral zone. This enormous loss of water provides an obvious explanation for their restricted ecological niche (Taylor, Spinage and Lyman 1969).

The impala (*Aepyceros melampus*) is a species which is periodically exposed to heat and aridity and it has been suggested that this bovid can also go without water for long periods (Lamprey 1963). Impala are medium sized mammals, weighing 55kg to 75kg and are distributed from southern Africa to central Kenya.

The impala is only partially bradymetabolic, its body temperature varying from just over 38° C at 20° C ambient temperature to over 40° C at higher ambient temperatures. Body temperatures can increase slightly, to over 41° C, at an ambient temperature of 50° C. Respiratory evaporation is more important than cutaneous water loss, the impala thus conforming to the small animal model. Respiratory frequencies are as much as 200 inspirations/min with open-mouth panting at ambient temperatures of 35° C to 50° C. Normal breathing rates are from 13 to 24 respirations/min at 22° C. Sweating rates at 50° C are $55gH_2O/m^2/h$ to $60gH_2O/m^2/h$ (Maloiy and Hopcraft 1971).

3.5 Independence of Brain and Body Temperatures and Counter-current Cooling

Elevated internal temperatures do not apparently cause harm to the majority of body tissues in desert-adapted animals provided that the rise is not more than about 6° C above the normal core temperature. Depression of central nervous system activity, particularly in the respiratory area, occurs before this (Schmidt-Nielsen 1975) and it is probable that such high temperatures would do permanent damage to brain cells.

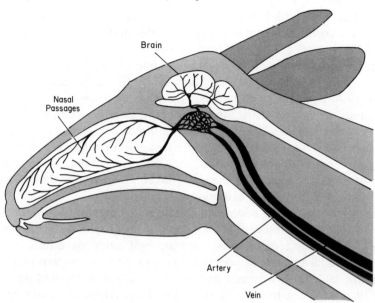

Fig. 3.13. The carotid rete and associated arteries and veins in the Beisa oryx (Taylor 1969a)

The carotid rete is a network of small blood vessels, breaking out from the carotid artery just below the brain in the cavernous sinus: it is not present in all mammals, but it is found in some species from both arid and non-arid areas. It was first noticed more than 2000 years ago by Herophilus, a Greek physician (Baker 1979), but modern interest probably dates from a detailed description during the 1950's (Daniel, Dawes and Pritchard 1953). In the region below the brain where the rete occurs, it meets with, and is surrounded by, the jugular veins carrying blood from the nasal region back to the heart (Fig. 3.13). The venous blood is cooled by the animal's panting and the lowered temperature of the air being exhaled through the nostrils and the mouth. The blood in the veins is thus cooler than the arterial blood being pumped from the heart and arriving from the opposite direction. This counter-current can result in blood entering the brain being reduced by as much as 3.9° C in Grant's gazelle (Taylor 1972). It is probable that counter-current brain cooling is better developed in animals that adopt the respiratory rather than the cutaneous evaporative route. It is also possible that some morphological alterations result, as in the long, trunk-like nose of Guenther's dik-dik.

The earliest reports of the physiological basis for differences between brain and body temperatures came from work on lizards (Heath 1964, 1966). In lizards it is suggested that a refinement of counter-current cooling in brain temperature regulation depends upon a combination of "circulatory adjustments" and "respiratory adjustments" In the former there is increased activity and a faster heart rate, while in the latter there are increased ventilation rates, the animal pants and there is sometimes gular flutter (Webb, Johnson and Firth 1972).

In mammals, early evidence for selective cooling of the brain came from goats (Taylor 1966), sheep (Baker and Hayward 1968) and in gazelles and oryx (Taylor 1969a). An abrupt rise in body temperature following strenuous exercise without a concomitant rise in brain temperature has been noted in antelope (Taylor and Lyman 1972), as well as in predators which prey upon them. It has, in fact, been proposed, as counter-current cooling is found in both arid and non-arid adapted animals, that the primary function of the carotid rete is to reduce heat after exercise (Baker 1979). The possibility of a dual function or of convergent evolution still remains.

The camel possesses a well-developed carotid rete, but early experiments in Morocco in a climatic chamber at 48° C failed to demonstrate any difference between body and brain temperatures. This apparent functional failure was ascribed to heat-induced nasal vasoconstriction. In a later experiment under field conditions (30° C), two female camels were studied at rest and when trotting at 10km/h. When hydrated and at rest, body temperature did not exceed 39° C and the brain was slightly below this at 38.0° C to 38.5oc. Hydrated camels subjected to exercise kept body temperature below 39° C by sweating, and brain temperature did not exceed 38.3° C (Fig. 3.14). In dehydrated camels body temperature was rapidly elevated to 40.5° C following exercise. Brain temperature remained at 38.0° C until it was forced to follow body temperature, but even then it did not exceed 39.0° C, that is 1.5° C below body temperature (Dahlborn et al. 1987). Camels are able to cool exhaled air to ambient or less than ambient temperatures as a result of the carotid rete, which not only further aids brain cooling but also enables

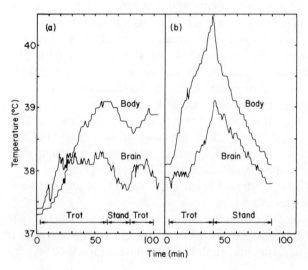

Fig. 3.14. Variation of brain and body temperature of the one-humped camel during excercise when *(a)* hydrated and *(b)* dehydrated (Dahlborn et al. 1987)

extraction of water from the exhaled air (Schmidt-Nielsen, Schroter and Shkolnik 1980).

In springbok, the only time at which body temperature exceeded the normal range was immediately after sprinting (Fig. 3.15), when it rose abruptly from 39.6° C to 41.4° C. It is considered that the thin coat of the springbok in relation to its predicted depth is an adaptation to that short, sharp burst of energy required to achieve sprinting speeds as high as or higher than those of the principal predators (Hofmeyr and Louw 1987).

Selective cooling appears to be an important physiological mechanism allowing animals to withstand high temperatures. It might be expected that, in animals with this faculty, anatomical and morphological modifications to increase the surface area available for cooling will also have taken place. Anatomical modifications do indeed appear to have occurred in some species. Long snouts, convex profiles and other facial changes result from these adaptive modifications. A comparison of the wildebeest and zebu cattle (Taylor, Robertshaw and Hofmann 1969) showed that the ratio of the splanchocranial length to neurocranial length was 5:2 in the wildebeest compared to 5:3 in the zebu, this difference accounting for the characteristic long-nosed, rather morose, appearance of the wildebeest. In the wildebeest

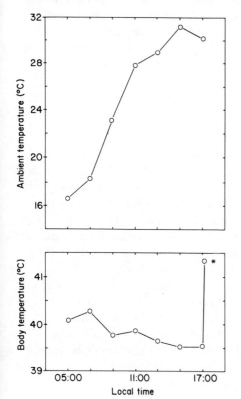

Fig. 3.15. Ambient temperature and springbok body temperature before and immediately after sprinting (Hofmeyr and Louw 1987)

Table 3.2. Respiratory passage measurements in wildebeest and zebu cattle weighing 130–140 kg (adapted from Taylor, Robertshaw and Hofmann 1969)

Character	Wildebeest	Zebu
Anatomical dead space[a] (ml)	630	450
Paranasal sinus volume (ml^3)	330	500
Area of frontal sinus opening (cm^2)	2.20	0.72

[a] excludes oral cavity, sinuses and alveoli

the length and the cross-sectional area of the nasal passages are greater than in the zebu and provide much more dead space (Table 3.2). The wildebeest has large openings to the paranasal sinuses which are directed orally to the incoming air path. In zebu cattle the openings are smaller and directed medially. Zebu cattle, such as the Africander, do, however, have a larger area of nasal sinus than temperate-type cattle such as the Friesland (Louw and Seely 1982).

Arid-adapted sheep and goats often have convex facial profiles which might be related to anatomical modifications to facilitate selective cooling. Other antelopes, such as the dik-dik, have long facial profiles similar in general appearance to the one seen in wildebeest. A possible behavioural mechanism to reduce the brain temperature is the habit of sheep bunching together with their heads under the bellies of their neighbours.

3.6 Pelage Characteristics

The importance of coat colour, depth and density has already been mentioned several times. It has recently been shown that the depth of the coat decreases in a log-linear manner in relation to body mass (Fig. 3.16), the power curve describing the relationship being d = 65M − 0.06, where d is pelage depth and M is body mass in kg (Hofmeyr and Louw 1987). Springbok, a small antelope, and steenbok (*Raphicerus campestris*), a very small antelope, had coat thicknesses that were significantly less dep than predicted by the sequation: both of these species are arid-adapted animals.

The relationship between pelage depth and conductance on a log-log plot was linear and gave a predictive equation of C = 0.74d + 1.42 for eight species, conductance being higher in heavier species with shorter coats. Domestic sheep had the lowest conductance of all the species studied. The springbok had a thinner coat with higher conductance than would be expected and therefore appears vulnerable to excessive wind speeds. Springbok probably compensate for this by having a lower absorption of short wave

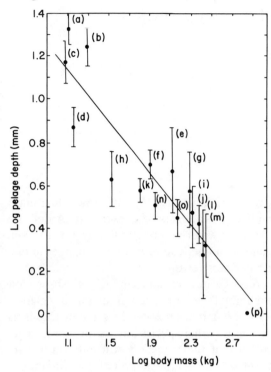

Fig. 3.16. The relationship between coat depth and body mass in 16 African ruminants (a) klipspringer; (b) vaal rib-bok; (c) grysbok; (d) steen-bok; (e) black wildebeest; (f) blesbok; (g) oryx; (h) spring-bok; (i) sable antelope; (j) blue wildebeest; (k) impala; (l) zebra; (m) kudu; (n) bonte-bok; (o) tsessebe; (p) eland; Hofmeyr and Louw 1987)

radiation, the value being 0.55 over the whole body surface (0.28, 0.60 and 0.66 on white, fawn and brown areas, respectively) compared to 0.71 for eland and 0.66 for hartebeest. Shorter coats in larger animals are probably an adaptation to the relatively smaller surface area in these species. The springbok is an exception to the general rule and has a thinner coat and higher conductance than predicted by its body mass. This probably results from selection pressure for heat dissipation after sprinting to escape predators rather than selection for a thicker coat which would provide insulation against cold and resist penetration of solar radiation.

4 Water Balance and Kidney Function

4.1 Introduction

Water is a scarce and precious resource in deserts. Animals (including man) and plants have evolved a number of strategies to conserve it. A delicate balance has to be maintained between water entering the body, metabolism, and water leaving the body. Changes in one lead to resultant changes in one or both of the others until the balance is restored.

The sources of ingress and egress of water are shown in Fig. 4.1. Absorption of water by the tissues within a mammal's body is through the salivary glands, the stomach and the intestines. Desert animals possess the same mechanisms to facilitate (or restrict) water loss as do other species but, as for thermoregulation, they have adapted them so that they function efficiently in a zone where the most bulky constituent of life is always limited and sometimes almost totally absent. In the long term, homeostasis has to be maintained if life is to continue, although it is not always maintained in the short term, especially if priority has to be given to thermoregulation and, in females, to lactation.

In most mammals, and under normal conditions, the main source of water is that which is drunk by the animal at more or less regular intervals. Secondly, and indeed in some cases primarily, water requirements can be obtained from

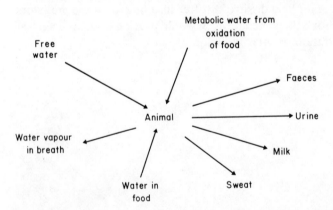

Fig. 4.1. The sources of water gain and water loss in a mammal

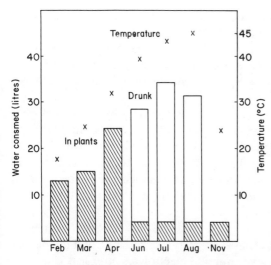

Fig. 4.2. Total water intake from different sources by camels in Mauritania at different times of the year (Gauthier-Pilters 1969)

Fig. 4.3. Dew drops on *Atriplex* sp. in Morocco

the ingested food; either from the water content of the plant eaten or from water condensed on the plant (Fig. 4.2). Condensed water, whether fog or dew, can be an important source of moisture for the animal (Fig. 4.3) in some areas at certain times of the year. Water from the metabolism of food or of some body tissues can also be important but may also be an unreliable source, especially when metabolism is reduced during dehydration or following extreme heat stress (Yagil, Etzion and Ganani 1978).

The relative importance of the routes of water excretion depends on a number of factors. The main routes are, however, by respiration from the lungs via the nostrils and mouth, perspiration via the skin, in urine and faeces and, in females, in the milk.

The amount of water that is lost is controlled mainly by the kidneys but depends also on the metabolic rate. Metabolic rate is an exponential function of body mass to the power of 0.75 ($W^{0.75}$). Water turnover is also an exponential function of mass to the power of 0.82 ($W^{0.82}$). Water turnover is therefore related to size and thus to metabolic rate. Where metabolic rate can be adjusted irrespective of body mass, then a lowered metabolic rate will result in a lower rate of water turnover.

Loss of body water can be tolerated to a greater or lesser degree by different species before physiological viability is lost. The rate and the degree to which animals can restore body water and electrolytes after loss is also an important adaptational function. Among mammals, the camel appears to be best able to tolerate loss of water and as much as 30% of initial body weight can be lost, apparently without ill-effects (Macfarlane et al. 1971). Some goats, in particular the black Bedouin type of the Middle East, can also tolerate high levels of water loss, but they lose it much more rapidly under the same conditions of climate and energy expenditure in comparison to camels (Shkolnik, Borut and Choshniak 1972). Man and a number of other animals can only tolerate a loss of water of as little as 10% of initial weight.

4.2 Water Requirements

Ruminants in deserts need to be able to tolerate very high air temperatures, heavy loads of solar radiation, often poor quality forage, and lack of drinking water. Factors influencing water loss include temperature and solar radiation from the foregoing list, the wind speed, the vapour pressure differences between the animal and its immediate environment, the nature of the skin and the animal's own metabolic rate and activity.

Water requirements of desert ruminants vary with the season and the temperature. During the short rainy season, free and preformed water in the food is usually available in sufficient quantities for problems of its conservation not to arise. In addition, the overall temperature is lower than during the dry season and there is some cloud cover which reduces the incidence of direct solar radiation. In the dry season, conditions are very different. Free water is usually scarce or completely lacking and preformed water is less, as a percentage of the total amount of food ingested, than during the wet season.

Table 4.1. Minimum water requirements (litres/100 kg live weight/day) for some wild and domestic ungulates when dehydrated to 85 per cent of initial body weight

Species Common and latin names		Number of animals in experiment	Temperature		Source
			22°C	22°/40°C	
Dik-dik	*Madoqua* sp	4	5.59	7.72	Maloiy (1973 a)
Thomson's gazelle	*Gazella thomsoni*	3	2.20	2.74	Taylor (1968 a)
Grant's gazelle	*Gazella granti*	3	2.08	3.86	Taylor (1968 a)
Impala	*Aepyceros melampus*	2	2.49	2.93	Maloiy and Hopcraft (1971)
Oryx	*Oryx gazella*	3	1.88	3.00	Taylor (1968 a)
Hartebeest	*Alcelaphus buselaphus*	3	2.98	4.04	Maloiy and Hopcraft (1971)
Wildebeest	*Connochaetes taurinus*	3	2.99	4.81	Taylor (1968 a)
Waterbuck	*Kobus defassa*	3	5.99	—	Taylor, Spinage and Lyman (1969)
Buffalo	*Syncerus kaffer*	3	3.43	4.58	Taylor (1968 a)
Eland	*Taurotragus oryx*	3	3.74	5.49	Taylor (1968 a)
Goat	*Capra hircus*	5	3.28	4.18	Maloiy and Taylor (1971)
Sheep	*Ovis aries*	5	2.66	3.22	Taylor (1968 a)
Temperate cattle	*Bos taurus*	3	4.62	6.42	Taylor (1968 a)

Heat loads from the high temperatures and from direct radiation are intense and the animal may compensate by reducing its food intake and being generally less active. Most animals also need to dissipate at least a part of the heat load by evaporative cooling.

An animal's size and its physiological, anatomical and behavioural characteristics in relation to that size are in large measure responsible for its ability to survive in arid environments, whether the aridity is continuous or intermittent. The minimum water requirements of some desert and non-desert ungulates under experimental conditions at moderate and at alternating moderate and hot conditions are shown in Table 4.1. The advantages of scale are in general clearly evident. Small animals, with larger ratios of surface area to mass have greater requirements for water than larger animals with smaller ratios: arid-adapted animals generally have lesser requirements than species such as the buffalo and the waterbuck, which require constant access to water. If water requirements are expressed per kilogramme of metabolic weight as opposed to actual mass, the advantages occurring to large animals are usually even more pronounced.

It is not clear how long it takes a species to become adapted to conditions of heat and water stress. It has been said that the evolutionary determination of water requirements probably occurred during the Pliocene (Macfarlane and Howard 1974) but basic physiological mechanisms can apparently evolve over a fairly short period. Zebu cattle, for example, were probably introduced into East Africa only about 4000 years BP (Payne 1964). During the intervening period several series of droughts have acted to kill off less adapted individuals and thus provided an environment conducive to severe selection prsssure. In the most recent years there have been, for example, severe droughts in Africa leading to large reported losses of domestic stock, particularly cattle. Droughts occurred across much of Africa in 1905 to 1910; in East Africa in 1961 (Taylor 1968a) and in 1982–1983 (Peacock 1984) and in West Africa in 1931 (Fuglestad 1974), in 1968–1973 (Temple and Thomas 1973) and again in 1984–1985 (Wilson, Hiernaux and McIntire 1989). The water requirements of zebu cattle can then be used to evaluate the speed at which water conservation mechanisms have evolved (Taylor 1968a).

4.2.1   Sources of Water

Water for animals derives from free water imbibed by drinking, preformed water in food, and the water obtained from the oxidation of food and body tissues, this last being known as metabolic water. Other generally minor sources of moisture (fog, condensation, etc) can be important in some areas and need to be included in calculations of total water availability.

In Sudan in winter Dorcas gazelle drank an average of about 470ml of free water per animal per day, equivalent to about 3.1% of body weight (Ghobrial 1970a). In summer the same gazelle drank 770ml, or about 4.5% of body weight per day. As already indicated (Sect. 3.4.3), Dorcas gazelle do require a constant supply of free water, when fed dry lucerne hay, both in winter, when they can effectively survive for 9 to 12 days without water, involving a weight loss of 14% to 17% of original weight, and in summer when they drink water every 3 to 4 days, losing 17% to 20% of initial weight over this period (Ghobrial 1974). The gazelle can replace lost water in one drink at the rate of 4.4 litres/100kg live weight to 10.1 litres/100kg live weight, about 6 to 11% of initial weight in winter. In summer as much as 7.6 litres/100kg weight to 17.0 litres/100kg body weight need to be drunk, about 8.4% to 23.1% of body weight. The Dorcas gazelle therefore has a requirement for free water under field conditions considerably in excess of the 1.3% of body weight required by the camel (3180ml for a 243–kg camel – Schmidt-Nielsen et al. 1956). It is, however, similar to the consumption of eland (4850ml for an animal of 100–150kg – Taylor and Lyman 1967) which, although much bigger, do not inhabit areas as dry as do the gazelle.

Unlike the camel and the Bedouin goat, the gazelle is not able to replace all lost body water at one drinking. Camels are exceptional, even among the

Camelidae, in being able to replace all (or almost all) of body water loss in one intensive drinking bout. A 600kg camel has been recorded as replenishing 200kg of water, accrued from a 14-day period of abstention, in 3minutes (Yagil, Sod-Moriah and Meyerstein 1974a). In contrast, the guanaco (*Lama guanocoe*), a South American high altitude camelid, was only able to replace about 67% of its accumulated loss of 13kg in the first 8-minute drinking session and took a further 2 days to equilibrate fully (Macfarlane 1964). Sheep are also able to restore body water loss in a very short period, as demonstrated by Merino sheep in Australia (Macfarlane, Morris and Howard 1962, 1963). Bedouin goats can also drink the total water lost very quickly (Shkolnik, Borut and Choshniak 1972), although the equilibration mechanisms differ between goats and sheep on the one hand and camels on the other.

It is evident that, in the Dorcas gazelle as well as in other species, the amount of preformed water obtained from food depends not only on the moisture content of that food but also on the amount eaten. In general, under colder winter conditions, energy requirements are higher and calorie intake can be increased by eating better quality food. It is more usual, however, to achieve greater calorie intake through eating greater quantities of food or food whose digestibility is high. If more food is eaten, more preformed water is available. In summer, conversely, appetite is lower and plants are probably drier, so less preformed water is available. Restricted access to drinking water, either experimentally or under field conditions, also generally depresses food intake, thus further exacerbating the loss of water available from food. In Dorcas gazelle, preformed water from food was equivalent to about 0.20% of body weight in winter but only 0.15% in summer, being about 30ml/animal/day in winter and 24ml/animal/day in summer. These intakes of water in food are much lower in relative terms than those achieved by the camel, for which it has already been demonstrated that almost all the requirements of water can be obtained from food over extended periods of time (Sect. 4.1, Fig. 4.2).

Metabolic water obtained from oxidation of food by Dorcas gazelle was equivalent to about 180ml/day (1.2% of live weight) in winter and 142ml/day (0.9% of live weight) in summer. For Dorcas gazelle, therefore, the

Table 4.2. Water formation and oxygen consumption and use in the metabolisation of various components of a food (Schmidt-Nielsen 1964)

Food element	Water formed (g/g food)	Oxygen use litres/g food	litres/g water formed
Starch	0.556	0.828	1.489
Fat	1.071	2.019	1.885
Protein	0.396	0.967	2.441

Table 4.3. Repartition of water input sources (per cent of total litres/100 kg live weight/day) in ruminants under different conditions of temperature and hydration (sources and number of experimental animals as for Table 4.1)

Species	Environmental conditions															
	22°C water ad lib				22°C water restricted				22/40°C water ad lib				22/40°C water restricted			
	Total Water	Per cent contribution			Total Water	Per cent contribution			Total Water	Per cent contribution			Total Water	Per cent contribution		
		D[a]	P[a]	M[a]		D	P	M		D	P	M		D	P	M
Dik-dik	5.6	70.0	10.3	19.7	3.7	72.4	10.9	16.7	7.8	78.2	8.2	13.6	4.6	72.1	11.1	16.8
Thomson's gazelle	—	—	—	—	2.2	56.8	10.4	32.7	—	—	—	—	2.7	77.7	5.1	17.2
Grant's gazelle	—	—	—	—	2.1	60.1	10.1	29.8	—	—	—	—	3.9	78.5	5.4	16.1
Impala	4.7	86.6	5.7	7.7	2.5	68.5	9.0	22.5	6.1	89.6	6.3	4.1	2.9	75.8	7.2	17.1
Oryx	—	—	—	—	1.9	69.1	9.6	21.3	—	—	—	—	3.0	70.3	8.0	21.7
Hartebeest	5.8	88.7	6.1	5.3	3.0	77.5	8.7	13.8	7.3	91.3	4.3	4.3	4.0	81.8	10.6	12.5
Wildebeest	—	—	—	—	3.0	74.6	7.7	17.7	—	—	—	—	4.8	85.7	4.1	10.2
Waterbuck	—	—	—	—	5.8	—	—	—	—	—	—	—	—	—	—	—
Buffalo	—	—	—	—	3.4	81.6	5.2	13.1	—	—	—	—	4.6	90.6	2.8	6.6
Eland	5.4	90.1	3.9	5.9	3.7	84.2	5.6	10.2	7.6	93.3	2.5	4.2	5.5	89.4	3.5	7.1
Goat	—	—	—	—	—	—	—	—	—	—	—	—	—	—	—	—
Sheep	—	—	—	—	—	—	—	—	—	—	—	—	—	—	—	—
Zebu cattle	—	—	—	—	2.0	82.6	5.1	12.3	—	—	—	—	3.2	91.6	2.5	5.9
Temperate cattle	6.1	91.7	2.8	5.4	4.6	89.0	3.5	7.6	7.7	94.4	1.7	3.8	6.4	94.2	2.3	3.4

[a] Drinking, preformed, metabolic

partitioning of sources of water gives about 69.1%, 4.5% and 26.4% of total water (680ml per animal per day) in winter to free, preformed and metabolic water, respectively. In summer, when the total water requirement was about 936ml per animal per day the proportions were 82.4% from drinking water, 2.4% from water in food and 15.2% from the metabolic water of oxidation (Ghobrial 1974).

The amount of metabolic water formed depends on the amount of hydrogen in the food, which in turn depends on the proportions of starch, fat and protein contained by the food. A small amount of hydrogen is not oxidised and, in mammals, most of this is excreted in the urine as urea (Schmidt-Nielsen 1964). Formation of metabolic water requires oxygen, the amounts needed being shown in Table 4.2. An increase in metabolic rate would lead to an increase in this amount of metabolic water formed, but this would be achieved at the cost of higher oxygen consumption. Expiration of air leads to a loss of water through the respiratory tract in proportion to oxygen use. Increased metabolism therefore usually results in a net loss, rather than a gain, to the body water pool. It can be seen from this explanation that a lowered metabolic rate results in a saving of water, as already described.

Some additional data on the partitioning of the sources of water available to an animal are provided in Table 4.3. These data are from confined animals under "simulated" desert conditions where temperatures were held constant at 22° C over the whole period of 24 hours or where a temperature regime alternating between 22° C for 12 hours and 40° C for 12 hours, to simulate desert night and day conditions, was imposed. The food provided was usually dry hay of relatively low water content and there was little if any opportunity for the experimental animals to select more succulent items, as they would almost certainly do under natural conditions. Under conditions of restricted water, all the species considered were able to reduce the proportion of free water in their total water requirements at both constant and alternating temperatures. Free water, however, still amounted to more than 60% of total water available at 22° C and usually to more than 75% under simulated hot desert conditions.

Many early explorers of arid areas reported that a number of animals under free-ranging conditions appeared to be able to survive without access to water (Sclater and Thomas 1894–1900; Roosevelt and Heller 1914). This belief is also inherent in the culture, folklore and national history observations of indigenous African peoples. A number of field studies have served to confirm the independence of free water, under natural conditions, of a wide range of animals from various habitats, if not permanently at least for extended periods of time. Such species include the dik-dik (Schoen 1972), the eland and the oryx (Taylor 1969a; Lewis 1977), Grant's gazelle (Taylor 1968b), the impala (Lamprey 1963), Swayne's hartebeest (*Alcelaphus buselaphus swaynei*) in Ethiopia (Lewis and Wilson 1979) and possibly Dorcas gazelle as well as numerous observations on the camel from several countries (Mares 1954;

Monod 1955; Davies 1957; Charnot 1958; Gauthier-Pilters 1958; Schmidt-Nielsen 1964; Cole 1975).

The strategies of most of these water-independent species are very similar. They comprise the reinforcement of physiological mechanisms with behavioural ones. Dik-dik have a food intake rate approximately twice that of cattle when converted to the same live weight, but they do not digest fibre very efficiently. In part, they overcome this problem of low digestibility by selecting rapidly fermentable food, but they also combine this with a series of short but frequent feeding and ruminating periods and a very short retention time of food in the digestive tract. This rapid passage enables relatively large amounts of food to be consumed and also increases the ingestion and retention of preformed water (Hoppe 1977).

Observations on eland have shown that they are nocturnal and crepuscular in their feeding habits under free-ranging conditons. They browse mainly at night and from just before sunrise to 10:00 h. They resume feeding in the late afternoon from about 17:00 h. During the heat of the day they avoid the worst effects of temperature and radiation by resting in the shade. Eland are essentially browsers and feed mainly on the leaves of *Acacia seyal*, A. *tortilis*, A. *reficiens. Balanites* spp. and *Grewia* spp. The moisture content of the leaves of these species is usually between 53 and 62%. Theoretical calculations, aasuming an average moisture content of 58%, an energy value of *Acacia* of 4.5kcal/g dry matter and energy values of 3.5kcal/g dry matter for *Balanites* and *Grewia*. a 5O% digestibility and a metabolic rate of 5000 kca1/100kg live weight/day, have shown that 3.6 litres of preformed water and 0.4 litres of metabolic water would be available per 100kg live weight for every 2.6kg of dry matter ingested (Taylor and Lyman 1967). This amount of water would enable an eland to fulfill all its water requirements at 22° C. At alternating temperatures of 22° C/40° C it would lose about 1% of live weight per day, but minor adjustments in feeding behaviour or a slight improvement in feed quality would certainly allow this deficiency to be overcome.

Oryx, which are mixed grazers and browsers, are also able to meet water requirements by feeding at night as well as during the day. The water content of even very dry plants can increase to as much as 42%, even when no dew is formed, as the temperature drops, causing the air to become almost saturated and allowing the plants to absorb water (Taylor 1968b).

Grant's gazelle in the northern dry regions of Kenya can probably also obtain all their water requirements from plants providing they eat at night (Taylor 1972). The dwarf shrub, *Disperma* sp., on which they mainly feed, contains only 1% moisture in the heat of the day but at night temperatures of 17° C and a relative humidity of 85%, the water content increases to 30% after 4 hours and to as much as 40% after 8 hours. Calculations of water intake based on twice the fasting metabolic rate (7.1 litres/O_2/kg/day), 50% dry matter digestibility, 4.8kcal energy/litre O_2 and O.54g metabolic water per gram digested matter, would yield water amounting to 3.10 litres at 30%

moisture content (just below the amount required at 22/40° C) and 4.12 litres at 40% moisture (slightly in excess of the amount required).

Using a similar method of theoretical calculation for Dorcas gazelle near Khartoum, it has been shown that a surplus of water of 600ml/100kg live weight/day could be obtained from food and metabolic water only during the cool winter period, but that a deficit of 1200ml/100kg live weight/day would accrue in the summer (Ghobrial 1974). The assumptions were that the *Acacia tortilis* leaves on which the gazelle fed contained 48% moisture, were not hygroscopic (or, if they were, this was for only a very short period during the brief summer rainy season), that the energy content of the leaves was 147 kcal/100g dry matter and that digestibility of the dry matter was 70%. In order to achieve the winter surplus the gazelle would need to consume 5.4kg dry matter per 100kg body weight and the summer loss would result from a consumption of 5.0kg per 100kg live weight.

In the Aïr and Tenere National Nature Reserve in Niger, Dorcas gazelle were most frequently observed in areas where *Acacia tortilis* was present. This tree, together with *Balanites aegyptiaca* and the herb *Chrozophora brocchiana*. formed the bulk of the diet. The perennial grasses *Panicum turgidum* and *Stipagrostis vulnerans* were not eaten and it was considered that this was because of their low moisture content (Grettenberger 1987). The dependence of Dorcas gazelle on feeds with a high moisture content is thus confirmed for almost all of their natural range.

Under free ranging conditions it is almost certain that all animals obtain much more of their total water requirements from preformed water in food than has been demonstrated in experiments designed to elucidate physio-logical mechanisms. The amount of preformed water actually obtained will depend on the choice by the animal of a favourable feeding habitat, selection of the most nutritious and moist plants, and selection of specific parts of plants. In semi-captive impala fed on lush green grass, for example, one animal obtained 71.4% (2.45 litres of a total of 3.43 litres ingested per 100kg live weight) of total preformed and drinking water from the food and another obtained 60.3% (2.05 litres of 3.40 litres) from food (Jarman 1973).

4.2.2 Dehydration and Rehydration

It has been demonstrated that a reduced water supply can be tolerated by a number of species of desert-adapted ruminants and that under these conditions use of available water becomes more efficient. Efficiency of use and tolerance of dehydration vary among species. In domestic animals kept under the same environmental conditions cattle lose water three times faster than camels (equivalent to 6.1% of body weight per day at day/night temperatures of 40° C/25° C) and sheep at two to two and a half times (4% to 5% of body weight). Cattle would die in 4 days at a total weight loss of

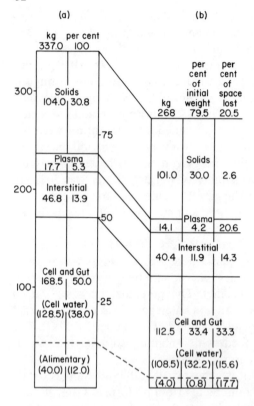

Fig. 4.4. Body composition of *(a)* hydrated camels compared to that of *(b)* camels after nine days without water (Macfarlane, Morris and Howard 1963)

28 to 32%, sheep in about 7 days, and camels would survive 15 or more days (Macfarlane, Morris and Howard 1962; Siebert and Macfarlane 1975), mainly because camels do not lose appetite with dehydration. Bedouin goats are capable of sustaining reductions in body weight of up to 35% (Shkolnik, Borut and Choshniak 1972) but lose water much more rapidly than camels.

The sources of loss for camels (shown diagrammatically in Fig. 4.4) are about 50% from the alimentary tract and intracellular spaces and 50% from the interstitial spaces with very little change in the water content of body solids and plasma. In cattle, losses are about equally divided amongst the body solids, the alimentary tract and intracellular spaces, and the interstitial spaces and plasma.

Animals that are fully watered usually contain about 16% of the body water pool in the plasma. Following dehydration cattle lose about 20% of plasma volume and the packed cell volume (PCV) rises correspondingly by about 20%: albumin concentration increases by some 8% and total protein by 29%. A major part of the camel's ability to withstand water deprivation arises from its ability preferentially to conserve plasma volume. Under severe dehydration plasma volume is reduced by only 5% (Siebert and Macfarlane 1971), the volume being maintained by absorption of water from the alimentary tract (Macfarlane 1964). In this situation in camels there may be a reduction in alimentary tract water of as much as 82% (Macfarlane, Morris and Howard 1963).

The control of water absorption from the intestines to the blood is probably under the control of ADH and aldosterone (Yagil and Etzion 1979). There is no concomitant rise in PCV in camel blood consequent on volume depletion, largely due to the peculiar resilience of camel red blood corpuscules (Peck 1939; Perk 1963), which are capable of reverting to their original size and shape even after severe compression. Camel erythrocytes are more resilient than those of any other animals yet examined (Perk, Frei and Herz 1964; Perk 1966). The erythrocyte count in the camel averages about 7.24 million per mm^3 of serum but rises slightly on dehydration (Banerjee, Bhattacharjee and Singh 1962). This rise is probably due to the longer half-life and survival time (12 days and 150 days) of red blood cells in dehydrated compared to hydrated camels (8 days and 120 days) and may contribute to water conservation (Yagil, Sod-Moriah and Meyerstein 1974a). Other work has shown higher counts of camel red blood cells, up to as many as 12.5million per mm^3 (Sharma, Malik and Saprea 1973), although the normal range appears to be from 4.2million per mm^3 to 10.0million per mm^3 (Ghodsian, Nowrouzi and Schels 1978; Yagil, Sod-Moriah and Meyerstsin 1974b).

Bighorn sheep (*Ovis canadensis*) also appear to have longer survival times of red blood cells in the wild in summer (204 days) and in zoos when dehydrated (203 days) compared to winter in the wild (155 days) and when fully watered in the zoo (197 days). The longer survival was thought to result from dehydration and heat stress (Turner 1984) and it is possible that this phenomenon is more widespread amongst desert ruminants than has yet been demonstrated.

Total protein increases are usually much higher in camels than in other animals, being as much as 70%, with a relatively greater rise in albumin of 20%. In Barmer goats in the Rajasthan desert total protein increases have been shown to be about 4% in dehydrated as opposed to hydrated animals, but the rise in albumin was of the order of 22% (Khan, Ghosh and Sasidharan 1978) the latter being significant while the former was not. In rodents, albumin has been shown to play an important role in survival following dehydration (Horowitz and Adler 1983). It does this by increasing osmotic pressure, thus attracting water, and it is probable that it has a similar function in ruminants.

When plasma volumes are maintained at or near normal levels, turgidity of the blood does not occur and the heart can continue to pump blood to the body surface and extremities, thus assisting heat dissipation and avoiding potential "explosive heat death" Other factors which play a role in maintaining plasma volume are also connected with the attraction of water. Glucose levels rise on dehydration, resulting in hyperglycaemia: the hygroscopic glucose then attracts water to the blood (Yagil and Berlyne 1977). Reported levels of blood sugar in camels vary over a fairly wide range of from 74mg to 140mg of glucose per 100ml of serum (Chavanne and Boué 1950; Kumar and Banerjee 1962; Maloiy 1972b; Yagil and Berlyne 1977). These levels are higher but also more variable than those found in cattle. Following infusion of glucose in dehydrated camels, levels in the blood increase but there is low urinary excretion, the converse being the case in fully watered camels. Insulin levels are also low in dehydrated camels, resulting from lowered thyroid activity and a reduced output of thyroid stimulating hormone (Charnot 1967).

Research in Israel has shown that during dehydration a rise in blood urea levels occurs (Yagil and Berlyne 1978b), as well as in levels of sodium and magnesium (Yagil and Berlyne 1976), but calcium and potassium levels are reduced. Increased levels of magnesium have not been found in every study and it is possible that this is due to differences in diets (Charnot 1961). Sodium levels rise as high as 202mEq/litre and potassium falls to 4.8mEq/litre (Macfarlane 1968).

In Barmer goats initial plasma sodium levels were higher than in dehydrated camels at 248mEq/litre, there being no significant change in goats following dehydration: there were also no significant changes in plasma potassium in the goats after dehydration (Khan, Ghosh and Sasidharan 1978). Similar changes have been shown in Indian desert sheep (Ghosh, Khan and Abichandani 1976; More and Sahni 1980).

Under normal conditions there are high concentrations of sodium in the camel alimentary tract (Maloiy and Clemens 1980), probably from the ingestion of salty plants. The camel alimentary tract thus acts as a reservoir for sodium. During dehydration, pH levels rise slightly, as does the pressurs of PCO_2 while PO_2 levels fall (Yagil, Etzion and Berlyne 1975). Haematocrit levels stay the same or decline. The fall in PO_2 levels might be due to the adaptive reduction in respiratory rate in dehydrated camels. There is more haemoglobin in camel red blood cells than in other species and this also has a greater affinity for oxygen than other species (Bartels et al. 1963). The ability of the high-altitude South American Camelidae to survive in oxygen-poor environments is related to blood cell morphology and intra-cellular haemoglobin concentrations (Yamaguchi etal. 1987). The changes in the blood gas composition of dehydrated camels result directly from the reduced respiratory rate and lowered oxygen consumption.

The increase in blood PCO2 and the reduction in PO2 should cause the blood to be more acidic but, as we have seen, pH is elevated and the blood remains alkaline, this being due to a reservoir of bicarbonate in the intestines (Maloiy and Clemens 1980), the uptake being under the control of the endocrine system. Levels of ADH in serum increase by as much as 340% in camels dehydrated for 10 days (Yagil and Etzion 1979) and it seems that the hormone also ensures the resorption of urea as well as water from the kidneys. As with glucose, urea is hygroscopic and its resorption into the blood acts as an additional water transfer agent. In sheep it has also been shown that urea, in addition to its role in increasing the glomerular filtration rate, acts to

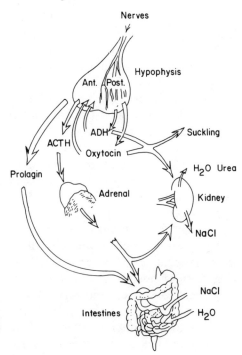

Fig. 4.5. Mechanisms of hormonal control of water metabolism (Yagil 1985)

promote greater resorption of water (Yesberg, Henderson and Budtz-Olsen 1973). Secretion of ADH is activated by aldosterone, but it is possible that the latter hormone also has a direct effect on water conservation. Prolactin and oxytocin, normally associated with release of milk (and therefore concerned indirectly with water requirements) are also possibly implicated directly in absorption and conservation of water (Fig. 4.5).

These changes in camel blood parameters have been interpreted as an acclimatisation to the conservation of body water under desert conditions but, in addition, they are able to provide a rapid response to acute non-physiological stresses to prevent loss of body water (Yagil, Sod-Moriah and Meyerstein 1974c).

Rehydration consists not only of the ingestion of water but also of its absorption and distribution throughout the body tissues. Ruminants in general, because of the large buffering capacity of the alimentary tract, ar* able to drink large quantities of water in a very short time after a period of privation. Animals without this capacity are rarely able to take all their water requirements at one short session, mainly due to the problems associated with haemolysis. Some non-ruminants are, however, capable of rapid drinking, including dogs and donkeys (Thrasher et al. 1981; Adolph 1981, 1982).

Amongst ruminants, camels (Hoppe, Kay and Maloiy 1975), goats (Choshniak and Shkolnik 1977, 1978) and sheep (Heckler, Budtz-Olsen and Ostwald 1964) are able to replace all the water deficiency and regain initial weight immediately the liquid becomes available. Cattle are not able to imbibe rapidly because of the dangers of haemolysis (Bianca 1970). There are many anecdotal reports of the huge drinking capacity of camels (Gauthier-Pilters 1958), as well as measurements in controlled experiments: the drinking of 200 litres in 3minutes after a deprivation period of 14 days to regain a weight of 600kg appears to be the record (Yagil, Sod-Moriah and Meyerstein 1974a). In goats, 3.27 litres have been reported as being drunk by goats averaging 15.8kg live weight after 4 days of dehydration, enabling them to recover 95.0% of initial body mass (Choshniak, Wittenberg and Saham 1987).

Even amongst the group of ruminants which drinks rapidly, the camel is peculiar in being able to absorb all the water almost immediately into the bloodstream. After 4 hours it appears that water is in equilibrum throughout most of the body tissues and normal intake resumes, if water is available. Renal function has also returned to normal after 4 hours and the erythrocytes return to their normal size and shape (Etzion, Meyerstein and Yagil 1984).

The resilience of the erythrocytes is probably largely responsible for the ability of camels to absorb water rapidly and to equilibrate after drinking large quantities. Normal dimensions of these red blood cells are in the range of $7.7 \mu m$ to $10.1 \ \mu m$ in length, $4.2 \ \mu m$ to $6.4 \ \mu m$ in width, about $50.6 \ \mu m2$ in area and $2.5 \ \mu m$ in thickness (Kohli 1963; Abdel-Gadir, Wahabi and Idris 1984). Consequent on dehydration for 7 days, the erythrocytes become relatively wider ($8.8 \ \mu m$ x $5.4 \ \mu m$) with an area of approximately $37.3 \ \mu m^2$. Within 4 hours of drinking, the cells have resumed their original shape and almost their original area (Yagil, Sod-Moriah and Meyerstein 1974b). Concurrently with this increase in size, a reduction in the number of cells per unit volume is observed, which is probably due to the dilution of the blood (Etzion, Meyerstein and Yagil 1984).

Following rehydration, camel blood chemistry parameters rapidly return to normal. Serum ADH levels drop, within 1 hour of drinking, to 86% below the original level, compared to the increase of 340% during dehydration (Yagil and Etzion 1979). This probably allows vasodilation to occur as ADH is also responsible for this function, hence its alternate name of vasopressin. At the same time as ADH decreases, aldosterone levels increase, this function being associated with the need to restore blood sodium to its normal level following large influxes of water. In sheep, blood sodium levels of 200mEq/l to 300mEq/l in dehydrated animals dropped rapidly to 10mEq/l to 50mEq/l following watering: this could lead to haemolysis and is the source of some reports that sheep cannot be included in the group of fast drinkers (Macfarlane 1964).

Goats are also among the species that can replace lost water rapidly at a single session. Water intake can reach as high as 45% of body weight without haemolysis resulting (Shkolnik, Borut and Choshniak 1972; Maltz and Shkolnik 1980). This peculiarity has been related to the role of the rumen as a store of water as, unlike in the camel, the water does not pass immediately into the blood and other tissues but remains for a considerable period in the alimentary tract.

After continuous grazing for 4 days in a traditionally managed Bedouin herd, five goats drank an average 4.58 litres, their dehydrated body mass being 16.3kg (Choshniak et al. 1984). Tritiated water (HTO) and Evans Blue (EB) spaces in the body were equivalent to 10.4 litres and 1.027 litres, respectively. After 12 hours the HTO and EB spaces had increased to 15.9 litres and 1.321 litres. A 3-fold increase in 51_{Cr} EDTA (a measure of rumen volume) was measured following drinking to satiety (Table 4.4). Following drinking, diminution of the rumen fluid during the first hour was only 1.5% of the original volume. Over the next 4 hours outflow from the rumen increased steadily and, at the 5 hour, was equivalent to a rate of about 5% of the volume at the start of each period per hour. After the expiration of 5 hours there was still 81% of the original volume in the rumen.

Increases in both osmotic and ionic concentrations in the rumen of these Bedouin goats occurred throughout the first 5 hours (Table 4.4). During the same period plasma osmotic concentrations were reduced by 29mOsm/kg and sodium (Na^+) and chlorine (Cl^-) were reduced, respectively by 9.5mM and 8.0mM, but potassium (K^+) and urea concentrations did not differ significantly after, compared with before, drinking. The results show that the controlled slow flow of water out of the rumen to the lower and permeable part of the gut, from where it is absorbed into the tissues, allows blood parameters to be maintained at near normal levels, thus avoiding overhydration and haemolysis (Choshniak et al. 1984). No increase in urine flow followed as a result of this relatively massive intake of water, indeed there was a decrease (probably in order to conserve the water imbibed) and a rate of flow equivalent to that of the dehydrated animals was not regained until 4 hours later. Low rates of urine flow following rehydration have also been noted in Merino sheep (Blair-West, Brook and Simpson 1972; Blair-West et al. 1979) in cattle and, of course, in camels (Siebert and Macfarlane 1975), but low rates in cattle were only transient.

Free water clearance remains in a negative ratio to osmotic clearance throughout the early post-drinking period (although osmotic clearance rates do drop in this time), thus demonstrating the role of the kidney in water conservation. Reductions in Na^+ and Cl^- clearance rates by the kidney also occur, but not as much as osmotic clearance. As a result, NaCl is preferentially conserved. When goats were allowed to drink a 0.9% solution of saline the outflow from the rumen was much greater, being 18% of the initial volume in the lst hour (556ml/h), this being followed by a gradual decrease in flow to 100ml/h in the 5th hour (Choshniak, Wittenberg and Saham 1987). Plasma osmolarity and urea concentrations dropped following drinking either of saline

Table 4.4. Ruminal fluid and blood parameters (mean ± s.e.) in black Bedouin goats dehydrated to 25 to 30 per cent of their initial body mass and following drinking to satiety (adapted from Choshniak et al. 1984)

Site and parameter	Unit	Before drinking	Time after drinking (h)			
			0–1	1–3	3–5	5–7
Rumen fluid						
Volume	ml	1738 ± 207	5227 ± 277	5091 ± 239	4585 ± 229	4260 ± 255
Osmolarity	mOsm/kg	328 ± 11	91 ± 7	111 ± 8	122 ± 10	131 ± 10
Na$^+$	mM	141 ± 3	61 ± 2	66 ± 2	73 ± 3	76 ± 2
K$^+$	mM	49 ± 1	18 ± 0.4	20 ± 0.4	21 ± 0.4	23 ± 0.4
Outflow	ml/hr	—	74 ± 36	211 ± 99	240 ± 34	—
Plasma						
Osmolarity	mOsm/kg	349.0 ± 5.0	343.0 ± 9.0	329.0 ± 6.0*	329.0 ± 9.0*	320.0 ± 9.0**
Urea	mM	15.7 ± 0.8	15.9 ± 1.6	14.2 ± 1.5**	14.4 ± 1.5*	15.3 ± 1.5
Na$^+$	mM	154.7 ± 0.8	156.5 ± 2.7	146.2 ± 4.3**	145.4 ± 4.6**	145.2 ± 3.0**
K$^+$	mM	3.7 ± 0.1	3.8 ± 0.2	4.0 ± 0.2	3.9 ± 0.3	3.8 ± 0.2
Cl$^-$	mM	126.0 ± 1.0	127.0 ± 3.0	122.0 ± 3.0	120.0 ± 4.0**	118.0 ± 2.0**

In the lower part of the table * and ** indicate significant differences, respectively at the 5 and 1 per cent levels, between the time after drinking and the level before drinking.

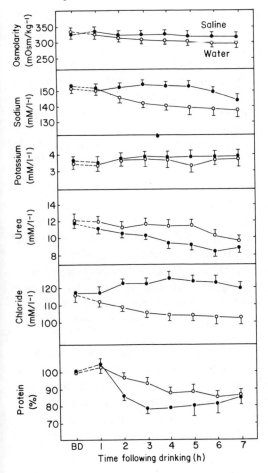

Fig. 4.6. Blood plasma concentrations after drinking saline (0.9 per cent NaCl) (●) of water (○) (Choshniak, Wittenberg and Saham 1987)

or of water (Fig. 4.6). Plasma levels of K^+ remained the same in both treatment groups, Na^+ and Cl^+ increased following imbibition of saline but dropped in the watered animals. Plasma protein remained stable at first but then dropped after 2 hours in the salinated goats to 85% and then 80% in the following hour: in the watered group there was a more continuous steady drop from the 2nd to the 7th hours (Fig. 4.6).

Outflow of rumen fluid was much greater in salinated than in watered goats immediately following drinking but, after 2 hours, there were marked reductions in the concentrations of plasma protein and urea, indicating an increase in plasma volume, although no changes in plasma osmolarity were observed. It seems that absorption of saline fluid from the rumen into the blood is responsible for an isotonic expansion of plasma volume, permitting a rapid restoration of water to the body, there being no chances of haemolysis after drinking saline as there is following the drinking of water (Choshniak, Wittenberg and Saham 1987).

In general terms, it seems unlikely that the end of drinking is determined by equilibration of the blood stream, as the camel appears to be the only animal that would respond to this signal. It is probable that satiation signals are passed to the hypothalamus from four sites. These four sites are: the pharyngeal area, the gastric area; some of the tissues recovering from dehydration; and volume receptors in the circulatory system (Adolph 1982). The relative importance of each site varies among species, but it is probable that in the camel the major ones are the pharynx and the rumen (Yagil 1985).

4.2.3 Effects of Dehydration on Appetite

One of the earliest and most important aspects of dehydration on metabolism is a reduced food intake. Even when food is in abundant supply a reduction in water intake inhibits and depresses the amount of food eaten. It is probable that there are two principal causes for less food being ingested. One involves a reduction in flow of saliva from the parotid glands and the other relates to changes in the rumen flora leading to less efficient digestion, particularly of nitrogen.

Heat stress alone, when water is still available ad libitum, is not a constant factor in the amount of food eaten. As can be seen from Table 4.5, some animals, including Thomson's gazelle, impala, oryx and arid-adapted sheep are capable of consuming more food when subjected to high temperatures than at lower ones. Other species, including Grant's gazelle, hartebeest, wildebeest, goat and cattle have reductions in food intake ranging from 10 to 50%.

Table 4.5. Food intake (kg food ± s.e./100 kg live weight/day) in ruminants under different conditions of temperature and hydration (Maloiy 1973 b)

Species	Number in experiment	Ambient temperature and animal water status			
		22°C		22°/40°C	
		ad lib	restricted	ad lib	restricted
Thomson's gazelle	3	2.65 ± 0.08	1.67 ± 0.04	2.56 ± 0.07	1.02 ± 0.06
Grant's gazelle	3	2.22 ± 0.05	1.53 ± 0.08	1.97 ± 0.08	1.51 ± 0.07
Impala	2	2.58 ± 0.06	1.99 ± 0.02	2.85 ± 0.04	2.15 ± 0.03
Oryx	3	2.23 ± 0.08	1.33 ± 0.05	2.25 ± 0.09	1.76 ± 0.10
Hartebeest	2	3.18 ± 0.02	2.70 ± 0.04	2.63 ± 0.04	1.99 ± 0.02
Wildebeest	3	2.09 ± 0.07	1.67 ± 0.04	1.80 ± 0.08	1.47 ± 0.05
Waterbuck	3	1.90 ± 0.09	1.61 ± 0.10	2.05 ± 0.09	— —
Goat	5	3.03 ± 0.08	1.27 ± 0.07	1.80 ± 0.15	1.21 ± 0.10
Sheep	5	2.55 ± 0.09	1.21 ± 0.10	2.87 ± 0.11	0.95 ± 0.02
Zebu cattle	4	1.62 ± 0.03	0.81 ± 0.03	0.80 ± 0.04	0.59 ± 0.04

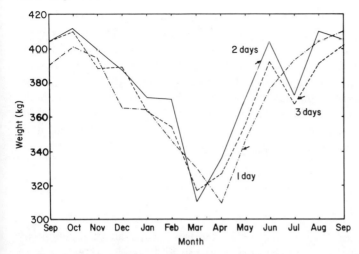

Fig. 4.7. Weight changes in lactating zebu cows in Ethiopia when watered at 1, 2 or 3 day intervals (Nicholson 1987)

When water stress is imposed and animals become dehydrated, food intake is reduced whatever the temperature. Under conditions of both heat stress and limited water there are further depressive effects on food intake, the reductions being particularly marked in the water-dependent species and in the domestic species of goats, sheep and cattle. Although food intake is reduced and weight losses occur in thirsty cattle (French 1956; Phillips 1960; Horrocks and Phillips 1961) recent experiments (Nicholson 1987) have shown that, at least in the medium term in arid-adapted zebu cattle, overall performance in terms of reproduction and subsequent compensatory weight gain is not affected (Fig. 4.7).

The apparent digestibility of the dry matter in the food can actually increase under water stress conditions, probably because nitrogen recycling and the use of urea become more efficient. When fed rations which supply only half of maintenance needs, however, zebu cattle watered once every 2 days reduced their fasting metabolic rate (by about 66 MJ Net Energy) much more rapidly than cattle watered daily, and thus saved considerable amounts of energy (Finch and King 1982).

In contrast to most species, the free food intake of camels does not decline markedly consequent on dehydration (nor does that of the arid-adapted donkey – Maloiy 1970). This is, of course, one of the major reasons why the camel is so widespread and so relatively productive in extremely dry areas. As already mentioned, reduced salivary flow is one of the principal factors resulting in lowered feed intake. In the camel there are well-developed parotid, maxillary and molar salivary glands, less well-developed sublingual glands at the base of the tongue, and some very small glands associated with the cheek papillae (Leese 1927; Nawar and El-Khaligi 1975). Under normal conditions of full water status, there is a rapid and copious flow of serous saliva from the parotid glands, amounting to about 21 litres/day per parotid gland (Hoppe, Kay and Maloiy 1974). Using normal ratios of parotid to total salivary flow would indicate that the camel produces about 80 litres/day when fully watered, this being reduced by 80% to about 16 litres/day when dehydrated. It appears that this amount of saliva is sufficient to maintain the appetite of camels under severe dehydration.

There is some evidence that at least some goats are also able to maintain appetite under conditions of heat and dehydration (Schoen 1968).

4.3 Water Turnover

Low rates of water turnover are a characteristic of arid-adapted ruminants. They allow longer times between drinking and thus enable better use to be made of sparse desert grazing. Factors which influence the body water turnover rate include the environmental conditions, total food intake and the type of food eaten, and the distance between the feeding area and the source of water. In suckling, young water turnover is influenced by the amount of milk drunk.

Most body functions can be related exponentially to $W^{0.73}$. The use of water is an exception and is related to $W^{0.82}$, where W is the live mass of the animal. The reason for the increase in the exponent is that water is used not only in intermediary metabolism but also for evaporative cooling. Different species have different rates of turnover but arid-adapted animals generally have lower rates of turnover than non-adapted ones. In general, however, there is a log-linear relationship between body water turnover and body mass. Some larger animals may use conservation measures related to their size and therefore may be an exception to the general rule.

Experimental data, some of which are shown in Table 4.6, are conflicting, and great variations occur within the same species in different experiments. These differences may result from differences in experimental design or from the actual amount of water available. It has been shown for desert mammals other than ruminants that the use of water and water turnover rates are highly correlated with the amount of water available to the animal (Kennedy and Macfarlane 1971; Hollerman and Dieterich 1973). There is also the problem that data obtained under experimental conditions are unlikely to reflect at all accurately the situation in the natural environment. Most experiments have also been carried out on animals under no other form of "stress" – pregnancy, lactation or work for example.

The little work that has been possible under field conditions has shown that lactating camels use water at a 50% higher rate than camels in general (Macfarlane, Morris and Howard 1962). Other work on the camel indicates

Table 4.6. Comparative water metoblism of some desert and non-desert ruminants

Species	Number of animals in experiment	Body weight (kg)	Body solids (%)	Water turnover/day		Source
				ml/kg l.w.	ml/kg$^{0.82}$	
Camel	4	520	30	61	188	Macfarlane, Morris and Howard (1962)
Camel[a]				93		Macfarlane, Morris and Howard (1962)
Dik-dik					83	Hoppe (1976)
Oryx	1	136	30	29	70	Macfarlane and Howard (1972)
Hartebeest	2	88	16	52	116	Maloiy anbd Hopcraft (1971)
Wildebeest	1	175	27	53	137	Maloiy (1973 b)
Eland	5	247	20	78	213	Maloiy (1973 b)
Goats	4	40	31	96	185	Macfarlane, Morris and Howard (1962)
Goats (Barmer)	12				118	Khan and Ghosh (1982)
Hair sheep		31	32	107	197	Macfarlane, Morris and Howard (1962)
Hair sheep (Magre)					227	Khan and Ghosh (1982)
Hair sheep (Awassi)	4	36	27	84	162	Degen (1977 b)
Sheep (Karakul)[b]	4	31	24	111	205	Maloiy (1973 b)
Sheep (Merino)[b]	6	38	29	94	180	Maloiy (1973 b)
Sheep (Dorper)[b]	6	41	31	88	170	Maloiy (1973 b)
Cattle (Boran)	4	197	23	135	347	Macfarlane, Morris and Howard (1962)
Cattle (Boran)	6	417	28	76	224	Macfarlane and Howard (1972)

[a] lactating
[b] all are arid zone breeds but the experiments were undertaken in hot and humid conditions in eastern Kenya

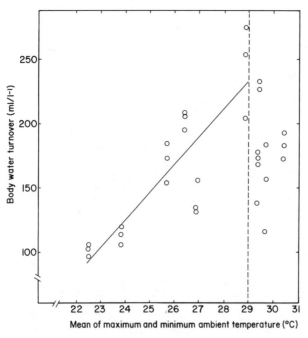

Fig. 4.8. Relationship between daily body water turnover and ambient temperature in zebu cattle under African ranching conditions (King 1983)

a turnover of about twice the standard, resting, rate for animals carrying heavy loads in the heat of the day (Schmidt-Nielsen et al. 1956). It has also been shown that young growing camels ranging freely on pasture used three times as much water as when they were confined (Macfarlane 1964). Low water turnover rates in heat-stressed and dehydrated animals are associated with the reduced metabolic rate of animals under these conditions (Macfarlane, Morris and Howard 1963).

The two most significant factors contributing to water turnover in animals at maintenance or under low production levels are that required for evaporative cooling and that required to ensure an adequate intake of food. Body water turnover rates increase with increasing heat loads, whether that load is measured in terms of temperature (Fig. 4.8) or directly in terms of solar radiation (Fig. 4.9). In zebu steers on natural grazing in a hot dry season the water turnover rate at 25° C is about 150ml/litre/day: at an average weight of 250kg and a body water pool of about 67% of live weight (that is about 168 litres) the absolute volume of water turned over would be about 25.2 litres/day (King 1983). At high temperatures (in excess of 29° C averaged over the 24h day) or under intense solar radiation (greater than about 475 W/m² to 500 W/m² depending on the species) the body water turnover rate might decline. The decline has been interpreted as being due to the animal's dissipating heat by evaporative cooling only up to a certain level determined by the turnover rate. Higher rates of turnover (in excess of 18% of the pool

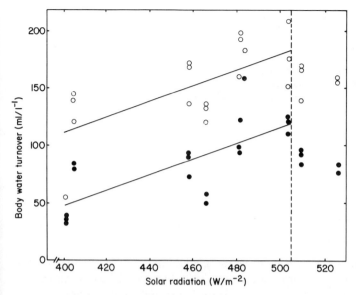

Fig. 4.9. Relationship between daily body water turnover and solar heat load in eland and oryx (King 1983)

in cattle and in excess of 24% in eland, for example) would lead to severe dehydration no matter how much water were available. A reduction in body water turnover rates at high heat loads implies that other forms of heat load are being reduced, that some other thermoregulatory functions are operational, or that some form of bradymetaboly is being used (King 1983).

As already stated, water turnover rates vary with environmental conditions within the same species of animal. This has been demonstrated in Kenya where there was a 2- to 4-fold variation between seasons (King 1979). There were also major differences between species in turnover rates, as can be seen from Table 4.7. Also shown in Table 4.7 is an indication of the body water pool for seven species of wild and domestic ruminants showing that sheep, with the least amount of body water, were the fattest species, and oryx and eland, with most water, were leanest. Using oryx as a standard it was possible to rank species in terms of the efficiency of water turnover (ml/litre$^{0.82}$ body water pool/day). Camels turned over water slightly faster than oryx, goats and sheep had a faster rate of use than the camel, while the eland, zebu cattle and buffalo all used water more than twice as fast as the oryx. It is probable that the more efficient use of water by the oryx is due in part only to the lower metabolic rate of this species. Most of the difference probably derives from the low requirements by the oryx for water for evaporative cooling.

More recent research in the Turkana district of northern Kenya (Coppock, Ellis and Swift 1988) has underlined not only species differences but also the

Table 4.7. Body water, water turnover rates and hierarchy of water use by seven species of ruminants in Kenya (adapted from King 1979)

Species	Body water pool (%)	Body water turnover (ml/kg/day)	Ratio of use (ml/l$^{0.82}$/day)
Oryx	73	30–124	1.00
Camel	72	38– 76	1.39
Sheep	60	62–167	1.74
Goat	65	76–196	1.82
Eland	73	66–177	2.12
Zebu cattle	65	63–178	2.39
Buffalo	66	108–203	2.62

changes in response of species to water availability in different seasons and there was a highly significant season x species interaction in water intake (Fig. 4.10). Rates of water consumption in camels were only 34% to 70% of those of other species and did not differ between dry and wet seasons. Consumption rates for donkeys did not differ between seasons but sheep (53%), goats (77%) and cattle (94%) drank much more in the wet season than in the dry. Cattle water consumption was increased in the wet season as a result of more frequent watering, while goats and sheep drank larger volumes at each drinking but were watered less frequently.

Species differences in TOH space and in water turnover are also apparent in cold desert mammals (Macfarlane et al. 1971; Macfarlane and Howard 1974). In the Taiga zone of central Alaska at 65°N, musk oxen (*Ovibos moschatus*) – described as a taiga camel – contain only 66% body water in their average weight of 324kg and had a water turnover of 35ml/kg/day or 99ml/kg$^{0.82}$/day in midwinter compared with three times as much for each of moose (*Alces alces.* 186 kg, 111 ml/kg/day, 284ml/kg$^{0.82}$/day) and reindeer (*Rangifer tarandus,* 100kg, 128 ml/kg/day, 293ml/kg$^{0.82}$/day).

Individual differences within species in rates of water and energy turnover are probably genetically determined (Macfarlane and Howard 1966).

In Awassi sheep in Israel the body water pool (expressed as TOH space) was much more than in sheep in Kenya, being 74.2% of total body weight in summer. It was demonstrated in the Awassi breed, as for domestic ruminants in Kenya, that seasonal differences existed, total body water in winter being 71.8% (Degen 1977a). Extracellular volume (SCn$^-$ space) also differed significantly between summer and winter, but plasma volume (Evans Blue:T$^-$ 1824 space) did not differ. It was considered that the maintenance of plasma volume was an adaptation to desert conditions, enabling a proper circulatory function to be maintained under severe heat stress. Water turnover varied with the saason and with the type of pasture. Lowest rates of turnover were noted

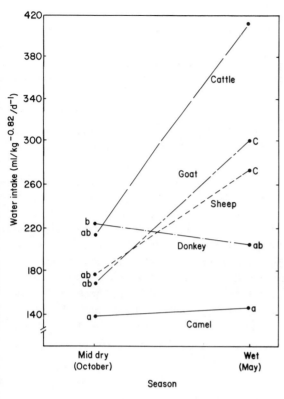

Fig. 4.10. Water consumption rates (ml/kg$^{0.82}$/day) for different species of livestock in Turkana district, Kenya in different seasons. Means accompanied by the same letter in the same season do not differ (Coppock, Ellis and Swift 1988)

when grazing dry native pasture (161.7 ml/kg0.82/day to 197.8ml/k$^{0.82}$2/day), but the turnover rate increased on good quality green pasture. Turnover rates were comparatively very high when feeding on saltbush shrubs (233.5ml/kg$^{0.82}$/day to 352.0ml/kg$^{0.82}$/day).

As part of the same series of experiments on Awassi sheep, total body water and water turnover were compared among dry females and pregnant or lactating ones (Degen 1977b). Total body water increased in pregnant ewes during the third and fourth months, indicating that body solids were being used for metabolism. At parturition, total body water was again reduced to low levels: the percentage body water dropped from about 77 just before parturition to about 72 after 1 month of lactation. Rates of water turnover increased during pregnancy although demand for pregnant ewes compared to non-pregnant ones differed only by about 10% at 4 months pregnant and about 11% at 5 months pregnant. In contrast, and as might be expected, lactating ewes had a much higher demand than dry ewes and turned water over about 29 % faster (303.1 ml/kg$^{0.82}$/day compared to 233.5 ml/kgv$^{0.82}$/day). The 29% increase is smaller than other domestic species, values of 109% being reported in goats (Maltz 1975 quoted by Degen 1977b), 44% in Australian Merino sheep and 44% to 51% in camels (Siebert and Macfarlane 1971; Macfarlane and Howard 1972).

Lactation makes the greatest demands on metabolic rates and on water requirements. Both water and energy requirements may increase by as much as 40 to 60% in temperate sheep (Brockway, McDonald and Pullar 1963). This level of increase is similar to the increased requirements of about 44% recorded for camels and Merino sheep in the arid zones (Macfarlane and Howard 1972).

Suckling young receive all their water requirements from the milk of their dams. Milk intake can be measured by the dilution of tritium, as milk intake is about 4% higher than water intake (the difference being due to the chemical elements in the milk solids). Water turnover is therefore directly proportional to milk intake. Very young animals have a total body water pool of more than 80%, but this reduces with age as suckling diminishes and a gradual transfer to solid foods is made.

Water turnover rates in Merino lambs have been measured as 1193ml/kg/day in singles and 1186ml/kg/day in twins in the first month of life when food intake is totally composed of milk (Macfarlane, Howard and Siebert 1969; Macfarlane and Howard 1974). As the lambs grew, water turnover rates dropped in both singles and twins, but turnover eventually became higher in twins than in singles, being about 10% greater at 1 month and 40% greater at 2 months. The total body water pool of twins remained higher than that of singles, due to an inadequate milk supply. The water cost of live weight gain was similar in both twins and singles.

4.4 Water Loss

The osmoregulatory abilities of domestic and wild ruminants, that is their ability to control water loss, have resulted in their being classified into three main physiological ecotypes (Maloiy, Macfarlane and Shkolnik 1979):

- High rates of water and energy use and poor ability to concentrate urine, usually from wet tropical or wet temperate zones – buffalo, cattle, eland, waterbuck, moose and reindeer [note that the elephant, pig and horse also fall into this group];
- Intermediate rates of water and energy turnover but with high renal concentrating ability, mainly living in semi-arid warm savanna – sheep, wildebeest and hartebeest [and donkey];
- Low rates of water and energy use with medium to high ability to concentrate urine and inhabiting the arid zones – camel, goat, oryx and most gazelle [and presumably the musk ox].

The mechanisms controlling water loss, and particularly evaporative heat loss, are probably centered in the hypothalamus and are triggered by heat sensors in various parts of the body. The sensors are located in many parts of the body, particularly in the skin, the central nervous system, the walls of the alimentary tract and in the hypothalamus itself.

Radiation, ambient temperature, wind speed and water or saturation deficit are the principal environmental variables influencing water loss. The major avenues of loss are through evaporation, in the faeces, in the urine, and in the milk of lactating females.

Evaporative water loss takes place via two routes, these being the cutaneous and respiratory ones. The relative importance of each of the evaporative sources of loss varies among species and may change within species in response to changes in temperature and in the state of hydration. In general, smaller species preferentially use the respiratory route while larger ones use the cutaneous one. Some indications of the relative importance of the two evaporative routes in different domestic and wild ruminants are given in Table 4.8.

In total, evaporative cooling can account for as much as 30% of the dissipation of the radiant heat load in the tropical ruminant and may be responsible for as much as 83% of total water loss (Taylor 1970a; Finch 1972a). Obligatory non-panting water loss through the respiratory tract and insensible loss of water from the skin are very minor components of water use.

Table 4.8. Relative contribution of respiratory and cutaneous evaporative water loss in some arid and non-arid adapted ruminants under various environmental conditions

Species	Relative loss (per cent)		Conditions	Source
	respiratory	cutaneous		
Camel	5	95	Hot, dry	Jenkinson (1972)
Cattle	35	65	Hot, dry	Jenkinson (1972)
Goat and sheep	60	40	Hot, dry	Jenkinson (1972)
Hair sheep (Kenya)	20	80	29°C, solar radiation	Gatenby (1979)
Bedouin goat	33	67	38°C, solar radiation	Borut, Dmi'el and Shkolnik (1979)
Waterbuck	55	45	22°C, hydrated	Taylor, Spinage and Lyman (1969)
Waterbuck	56	44	22°C, dehydrated	Taylor, Spinage and Lyman (1969)
Waterbuck	37	63	22°C/40°C, hydrated	Taylor, Spinage and Lyman (1969)
Eland	20/30	80/70	22°C/40°C, hydrated	Taylor and Lyman (1967)
Eland	22	78	22–32°C	Finch (1972 b)
Hartebeest	62	38	22–32°C	Finch (1972 b)
Dorcas gazelle	12	88	26–30°C	Ghobrial (1970 a)
Dik-dik	95 (?)	5 (?)		Hoppe (1977)

In all cases so far studied, evaporative loss exceeds faecal and urinary losses combined. When animals are dehydrated the reduction in loss via the evaporative routes is always at least equal to the reduced output in faeces and urine, but is usually relatively greater.

4.4.1 Respiratory Evaporation

Many animals respond to a hot environment by resorting to an increased respiration rate and, in some cases, to open-mouth panting. The increased respiration rate is usually accompanied by a reduced tidal volume, an increase in alveolar volume, a decrease in the arterial partial pressure of carbon dioxide (PCO_2) and an increase in the respiratory minute volume.

The oxygen cost of panting appears to be rather low in most ruminants. Panting appears to be a more efficient method of evaporative cooling than sweating, and it is probably for this reason that it is adopted by smaller ruminants. In addition to using the latent heat in the deep body, panting takes advantage of the airflow it creates over the moist surfaces of the lungs, respiratory tract and the mouth. When an animal sweats, electrolytes and salt are lost with the water, but they are not lost via the respiratory route, especially if saliva is not allowed to escape. In addition, panting assists in cooling the nasal and oral passages through which the venous blood returns via the rete and helps to cool the brain (Sect. 3.5).

Disadvantages associated with panting include the risk of blood alkalosis due to the build up of PCO_2 and an increase in work, and therefore additional heat production, by the muscles involved in respiration. The panting rates of some ruminants at various temperatures and under different conditions of water balance are shown in Fig. 4.11.

It has already been demonstrated (Sect. 3.2) that respiration rates in the camel increase very little with an increase in ambient heat load and the respiratory route is a very minor source of water loss. In addition, camels are able to exhale unsaturated air under some conditions (Schmidt-Nielsen, Schroter and Shkolnik 1980). At a day body temperature of 40° C the exhaled air is fully saturated but at a night body temperature of 36° C and with the exhaled air at 25° C the relative humidity is only 75%. The combination of cooling and desaturation can result in a saving of 60% of the water that would be present in fully saturated air exhaled at body temperature. A lower rate of breathing at night also increases the tidal volume of air and the amount of oxygen extracted, thus further reducing water loss. The only other large animal which has been recorded as being able to expire unsaturated air is the ostrich (Withers, Siegfried and Louw 1981) although the phenomenon is well known in small rodents (Jackson and Schmidt-Nielsen 1964).

In zebu cattle, which normally lose most water by sweating (Table 4.8), the respiratory rate remains low even at temperatures approaching 50° C. In dehydrated animals the increase in the respiratory rate began later than in

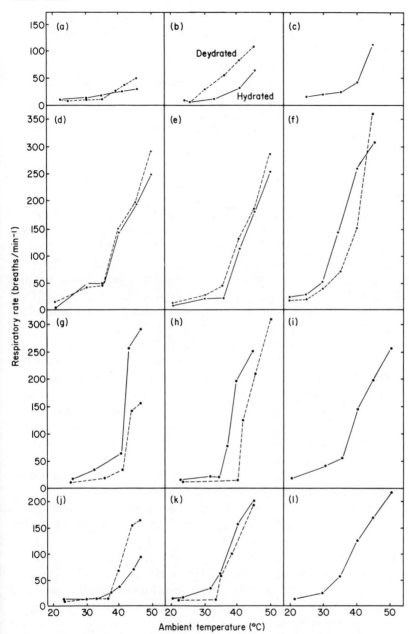

Fig. 4.11. Respiratory rates of ruminants under various conditions of temperature and water balance (● – – – ● dehydrated; x ——— x hydrated: *(a)* zebu steer, Taylor 1970 b; *(b)* buffalo, Taylor 1970 b; *(c)* waterbuck, Taylor, Spinage and Lyman 1969; *(d)* goat, Maloiy and Taylor 1971; *(e)* hair sheep, Maloiy and Taylor 1971; *(f)* dik-dik, Maloiy 1973 a; *(g)* Grant's gazelle, Taylor 1970 b; *(h)* Thomson's gazelle, Taylor 1970 b; *(i)* impala, Maloiy and Hopcraft 1971; *(j)* oryx, Taylor 1970 b; *(k)* wildebeest, Taylor 1970 b; *(l)* hartebeest, Maloiy and Hopcraft 1971)

hydrated animals, but at 45° C was higher in the former group than in the latter (Taylor 1970b). The difference between the two groups was not, however, very great and the maximum rate did not exceed 40 respirations/min in dehydrated animals and 30/min in hydrated ones.

In another experiment on zebu cattle, respiration rate increased from about 40 to almost 150 breaths/min as ambient temperature rose from 40° C to 50° C (Taylor, Robertshaw and Hofmann 1969). Tidal volume decreased with increasing respiration rate from about 1.8 litres/respiration at 16 respirations/min to about 1.0 litres/respiration at 58 respirations/min. At the same time alveolar volume increased from 20 to 54 litres/min while oxygen consumption increased from just under 4 litres/kg/day to about 6 litres/kg/day which could be explained entirely by the Q_{10} effect.

In East African goats and sheep, in which evaporative water loss is slightly greater via the respiratory than via the cutaneous route (Table 4.8), respiration rates increased very markedly from about 15 to 20 breaths/min at 20° C to between 250 and 300 breaths/min at 50° C (Fig. 4.11). Dehydration had little effect on the change in respiration rate, this being similar in both fully watered and water-deprived animals: this has been interpreted as meaning, at least partly, that goats and sheep do not have the physiological mechanisms required to survive in hot deserts without water (Maloiy and Taylor 1971).

Other types of goats may, however, be better adapted than East African animals. Bedouin goats in Israel showed a markedly reduced respiration rate when deprived of water and this was accompanied by a reduced oxygen consumption at higher temperatures coupled with a low metabolic rate (Shkolnik, Borut and Choshniak 1972). A reduced metabolic rate results in less endogenous heat production and less water is therefore required for evacuating heat, this being in addition to reducing lung ventilation and the amount of food needed for survival.

Larger mammals usually sweat to dissipate heat. Among the domestic species, both camels and cattle have adopted this strategy. Among wild species living in or close to deserts the ruminants which use the cutaneous route of evaporative cooling include buffalo, eland and, under some circumstances, oryx.

At low air temperatures and at deep body (rectal) temperatures of about 36° C the number of respirations/min in the eland is only about 8. This rate increases to about 15 or 16 in eland whose rectal temperature is raised to 39° C. At lower ambient and therefore lower rectal temperatures there are changes in all the parameters. In an experiment in which ambient temperature varied from 22° C to 14° C there was a 16% to 17% reduction in respiration rate and increases of 23% in tidal volume, 18% in oxygen extraction and 19% in oxygen consumption. The alveolar (ventilation) volume increased only slightly by about 2% (Taylor 1969b), this figure not being statistically significant.

The eland succeeds in maintaining its body temperature at a relatively low level, because of thermal inertia due to its large mass, until quite late in the day (Sect. 3.4.1). At sustained high ambient temperatures the respiration rate increases considerably and does so rather rapidly from about 25 to about 50 breaths/min (Finch 1972a). About 28% of total evaporative heat loss in the eland is via the respiratory route (Table 4.8).

Evaporative heat loss in elands only dissipates, however, about 31% of the effective radiative heat load, most of the remainder being lost as re-radiated long wave emission from the fur surface (Finch 1972b). Respiratory heat loss therefore contributes about 10% of the total heat lost. As in this camel, lower night body temperatures in the eland also enable air to be exhaled at a lower temperature. Although there is no evidence that eland exhale desaturated air, the saving in water between air saturated at a typical day body temperature of 39° C and a night temperature of 34° C would be about 25% (Taylor 1969a).

Buffalo reduce the heat load from the environment mainly by sweating. In fully hydrated buffalo the respiration rate begins to rise from very low levels at about 32° C, but the rate remains relatively slow and does not exceed 70 breaths/min at 45° C (Fig. 4.11). When dehydrated, the rate begins to increase at a lower temperature but does not exceed 110 respirations/min at 45° C.

The waterbuck dissipates heat in approximately equal proportions from both the respiratory and cutaneous routes (Table 4.8). It can be considered an intermediate species between those that dissipate heat mainly by panting and those that dissipate it mainly by sweating. The respiratory rate did not show an abrupt change at any one temperature (Fig. 4.11), but gradually increased when the temperature was about 35° C, to reach a maximum of about 120 breaths/min at 45° C (Taylor, Spinage and Lyman 1969). Oxygen consumption in both hydrated and dehydrated waterbuck was similar at about 6.4 litres O_2/kg/day over a rather wide thermoneutral zone of 13° C. These results confirm the supposition that the waterbuck, although found in favourable microhabitats within the arid zone, is not an arid-adapted ruminant. In order to be better adapted, the waterbuck could reduce respiratory evaporation by reducing its metabolism and respiring less air, by increasing oxygen extraction from the inhaled air, or by expiring unsaturated air, but the animal does not, even when dehydrated, exploit any of these mechanisms.

The oryx appears to be a problem species in respect of its evaporation strategies. The same authority has described it both as primarily a respiratory evaporator (Taylor 1969a) and as a cutaneous evaporator (Taylor 1970b). It is probable that the oryx adopts different strategies depending on its water status. When dehydrated, it uses the less expensive respiratory path, with a rhythm of up to 200 breaths/min at temperatures of about 45° C, compared with a rhythm of only about 100 breaths/minute when hydrated (Fig. 4.11). It maintains a low rate of sweating when dehydrated but sweats rather profusely when fully hydrated.

The hartebeest (Table 4.8), wildebeest and impala (Fig. 4.11) are all primarily respiratory evaporators. In hydrated hartebeest, the respiration rate is maintained at low rates while temperatures are low, but the number of breaths/min rises rapidly at ambient temperatures above 35° C to reach about 220 at 50° C (Maloiy and Hopcraft 1971). The impala has a similar response although at very high ambient temperatures the respiratory rate exceeds 250/min. In both the hydrated and dehydrated states wildebeest show a rapid acceleration in the respiration rate when temperatures exceed 35° C, the pattern being similar whether or not the animal has access to water, a maximum rhythm of about 180 to 200 respirations/min being reached at 45° C (Taylor 1970b).

Most of the medium- to small-sized gazelle are also respiratory evaporators although there are minor differences, especially between Thomson's gazelle and Grant's gazelle in their responses to hydration and dehydration (Fig. 4.11). The respiratory rate of Thomson's gazelle does not exceed 250 breaths/min when hydrated, but exceeds 300 breaths/min when dehydrated, especially at very high temperatures of 50° C. In contrast, Grant's gazelle has a higher respiratory rate when hydrated than when dehydrated (Taylor 1970b, 1972). At very high temperatures of 45° C and above, Grant's gazelle uses less water than does Thomson's because of its ability to allow its body temperature to rise above the ambient, an ability which the Thomson's gazelle does not possess (Taylor 1972). The springbok resorts to open-mouth panting at a rhythm approaching 300 respirations/min at high ambient daytime temperatures (Hofmeyr and Louw 1987).

The Dorcas appears to be the exception to the small animal model among gazelle (Table 4.8). Most heat is dissipated by evaporation via the cutaneous route, but the temperatures at which the observations were made were not as high as those to which other antelope were subjected. At 28° C and 45% relative humidity the respiration rate was 45 to 55 breaths/min and at 29° C and 30% humidity it was 50 to 75 breaths/min (Ghobrial 1970a).

The respiration rate of the dik-dik starts to rise shortly after the ambient temperature reaches 30° C (Figure 4.11), to reach 310 breaths/min in hydrated animals and about 370 breaths/min in dehydrated ones (Maloiy 1973a). The tidal volume of air at rapid respiration rates is greatly reduced and in the dik-dik only the respiratory dead space is ventilated. Arterial blood is thus diverted to the moist mucous membranes of the oral and nasal cavities where the rapid inhalation and exhalation of air causes moisture to evaporate, consequently cooling the blood. The condensed moisture is actively licked by the dik-dik in order to increase the total amount of water available (Hoppe 1977). It is possible that the long muzzle of this small antelope is an anatomical adaptation to assist the physiological process of water conservation.

At the high rates of panting in the dehydrated dik-dik, there is obviously considerable activity demanded of the respiratory muscles and it might be considered that there is some energy cost involved. Oxygen consumption is, however, as much as 42% lower in panting dik-dik than in thermoneutral dik-dik at rest (Hoppe et al. 1975). This is in contrast to a 13% to 40% increase in oxygen uptake in eland (Taylor and Lyman 1967) and a 50% increase in oxygen uptake at the start of panting in wildebeest (Taylor, Robertshaw and Hofmann 1969).

4.4.2   Cutaneous Evaporation

Some water moves through the skin of most mammals by insensitive diffusion. Most of the water which passes through the skin, however, does so in the form of active sweating. There is still need to clarify further the regions of the body which sense temperature and thus initiate the onset of sweating. The relative importance of peripheral and central temperature receptors also needs additional study.

Most species of mammals possess sweat glands, but their activity varies greatly. Sweat glands are tubular in shape and comprise a body and a long straight duct. Sweat glands are always associated with a hair follicle, but the reverse is not necessarily the case. Sweat glands in camels, goats and sheep are associated only with large primary hairs, while in cattle and buffalo each hair follicle has a sweat gland (Jenkinson 1972).

There are species differences in the number of sweat glands per unit area. In domestic animals there are differences between breeds and between individuals within breeds. Variations in sweat gland density and shape explain only part of the differences in the efficiency of sweating. On a single animal with a similar density of sweat glands over the whole body there are regional differences in water loss from evaporation.

Different methods of sweat gland function result in different patterns of evaporative water loss from both domestic and wild ruminants (Fig. 4.12). There are three distinct types of sweating in ruminants. These are an intermittent synchronous discharge (goats, sheep, oryx and gazelle), a stepwise increase (cattle, buffalo) and a steady increase on exposure to hotter environments (camel and llama *(Lama glama)*, eland and waterbuck). Although output from an individual sweat gland in different species may be similar when sweat is actually being discharged, it will be obvious that the pattern of sweating has a major role in the total evaporative heat loss. The efficiency of sweating also depends on the sustainability of the output and on the delay in its onset. Dehydration usually results in the onset of sweating being delayed and in the total amount of sweat being reduced (Fig. 4.13).

The sympathetic nervous system is involved in the control of sweating (Jenkinson 1972) although the sweat glands of most species do not appear

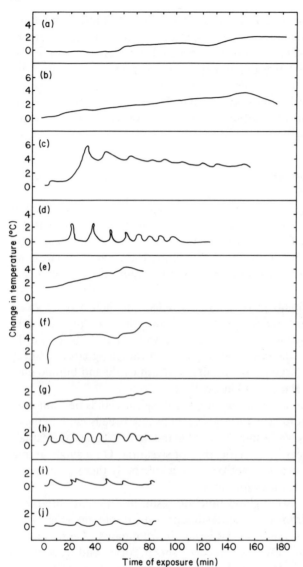

Fig. 4.12. Patterns of cutaneous moisture loss in various domestic and wild ruminants when exposed to a dry bulb temperature of 23°C *(a)* camel, Jenkinson 1969; *(b)* cattle, Jenkinson 1969; *(c)* sheep, Robertshaw 1968; *(d)* goat, Jenkinson and Robertshaw 1971; *(e)* eland, Robertshaw and Taylor 1969; *(f)* buffalo, Robertshaw and Taylor 1969; *(g)* waterbuck, Robertshaw and Taylor 1969; *(h)* oryx, Robertshaw and Taylor 1969; *(i)* Grant's gazelle, Robertshaw and Taylor 1969; *(j)* Thomson's gazelle, Robertshaw and Taylor 1969)

to be innervated. There should therefore be some peripheral mechanism acting between the nerve endings and the sweat glands. As most species respond to adrenalin in terms of sweat output, it is probable that this hormone acts as a transmitter substance.

Temperature differences between the deep body and the surface result in changes in the rate of blood flow. Heat loss through the skin is related to the difference between these two sites and the tissue conductance. The effects of cooling result from changes in the skin temperature, which depends on the

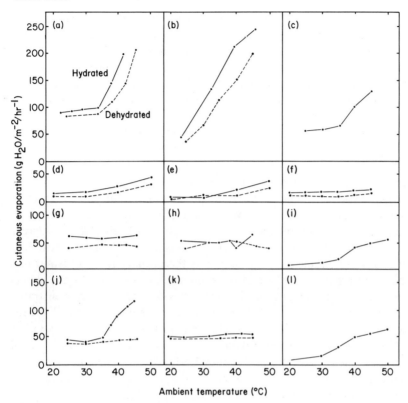

Fig. 4.13. Cutaneous moisture loss of ruminants under various conditions of temperature and water balance (● – – – ● dehydrated; x _____ x hydrated: species and sources are as for Fig. 4.11.)

core and ambient temperatures as well as the rate at which water is evaporated from the skin. As we have seen, wind speed is an important factor in the overall equation. Skin temperature is not, therefore, the only variable controlling the sweating rate. Other factors involved in sweat control include metabolic rate, tissue insulation and rectal temperature. Animals that use sweating as the main means of evaporative cooling are unable to overcome heat stress when the heat load is so high that the sweating rate has already reached its maximum or when (a rare case in deserts) the ambient humidity is too high to allow evaporation of the sweat produced.

The main source of evaporation in the camel is via the skin. A characteristic of the camel is that there is no copious flow of sweat or obvious wetting of the fur (Schmidt-Nielsen et al. 1957b). The evaporation takes place at the surface of the skin and not at the extremities of the fur, and the latent heat of evaporation is therefore drawn from the skin rather than from the atmosphere.

The effect of the fur as a heat barrier has been demonstrated by comparing two camels, one of which was clipped and the other not: the unclipped camel used only about 65% of the water that was turned over by the clipped camel. The rate of evaporation of the camel increases linearly when temperatures exceed 35° C, the maximum of $280gH_2O/m^2/h$ being reached at about 55° C. The South American camelid, the llama, has a similar rate of sweating of $250gH_2O/m^2/h$ at elevated temperatures.

Sweat glands in the camel are simple in structure and distributed over the whole body except in the upper lip, nose and the perianal region. On average, there are 200 glands/cm^2. Camel sweat contains about 40mEq/litre of potassium and 9.5mEq/litre of sodium: the pH varies from 8.2 to 8.4 (Macfarlane 1964). The high content of potassium (mainly in the form of $KHCO_3$) has been considered by Macfarlane (1964) to be due to the high potassium content of the plants eaten by camels, but Yagil (1985) disagrees with this and contends that the electrolyte levels are hormonally controlled.

Cattle also use cutaneous evaporation as the primary route of water loss in temperature regulation. The relative proportion evaporated by the skin is not as great as in the camel (Table 4.8) but it has recently been demonstrated that the rate of sweating in cattle of both temperate and tropical breeds increases exponentially in relation to skin temperature (Gatenby 1986). Other studies have shown a better relationship of sweating rate with rectal temperature (Finch, Bennett and Holmes 1982). Sweat glands in cattle may be present at a density of as much as 2000/cm^2 and a maximum sweating rate of $200gH_2O/m^2/h$ has been recorded for zebu types (Fig. 4.13).

Domestic small ruminants normally conform to the small animal model of evaporative cooling and more water is lost through the respiratory tract than via the skin. Both goats and sheep have a similar number of sweat glands, these being present in the order of 175/cm^2 to 250glands/cm^2. In both species the pattern of discharge is very similar, there being discrete peaks at fairly regular intervals, although there is a rapid fall off in activity due to fatigue in goats. Cutaneous evaporation is higher in hydrated animals of both species than it is in dehydrated ones, but maximum discharge rates do not exceed $40gH_2O/m^2/h$ in either species. The sweat of Merino sheep has about the same pH (8.2–8.5) as that of camels, but the potassium:sodium ratio is wider at about 20:1.

An exception to the general rule governing domestic small ruminants appears to be the black Bedouin goat of the Middle East. This breed has a sweat rate which, at about $140gH_2O/m^2/h$, approaches that of many cattle. This increased rate is due to a greater secretory capacity of individual glands, as the gland density is similar to that in other breeds of goat. The mechanism of secretion is not known, as the glands of the Bedouin goat do not differ histologically from those of other breeds (Dmi'el, Robertshaw and Choshniak 1980). It is possible that the Bedouin goat, which appears to have opted for the cutaneous route of water loss, is better adapted to desert conditions in this respect than other types of small ruminants.

The eland dissipates most of its environmental heat load by sweating and responds to increased heat load by a more or less constant increase in the sweating rate (Table 4.8, Fig. 4.12). Changes in both panting and sweating in the eland are closely related to skin temperature and the change occurs very rapidly at skin temperatures of 33° C. The skin temperature remains, however, lower than deep body temperature: the ability of the eland to store large amounts of heat (and thus save water) because of its size is again evident and the core temperature continues to rise well after sweating has stopped. Cutaneous evaporation rates rise from about $100gH_2O/m^2/h$ during the early part of the day to more than $400gH_2O/m^2/h$ for 2 or 3 hours from 11:00 h (Finch 1972a). As the deep body temperature is always higher than the skin temperature, all the heat flowing outwards (as well as a part of the metabolic heat) is lost by sweating. Most of the latent heat of evaporation comes from the environment rather than from the skin.

Under fairly low ambient heat loads, buffalo show an immediate and massive response (Fig. 4.12) by increasing the rate at which they sweat (Fig. 4.13). In hydrated buffalo the cuteneous respiration rate rose rapidly from below $50gH_2O/m^2/h$ at 20° C ambient temperature to about $250gH_2O/m^2/h$ at 45° C (Robertshaw and Taylor 1969; Taylor 1970b). Dehydrated buffalo sweat slightly less copiously than hydrated ones, but rates still reach $200gH_2O/m^2/h$. The high and sustained rate of water loss serves to underline the fact that buffalo that venture into arid or semi-arid areas must have constant recourse to a favourable micro-environment where green grass and a plentiful water supply are available.

The waterbuck evaporates water in approximately equal proportions via the respiratory and cutaneous routes (Table 3.8). The basal sweating rate is fairly high, in excess of $50gH_2O/m^2/h$, and this increases at ambient temperatures in excess of 35° C to achieve a level of between $130gH_2O/m^2/h$ and $140gH_2O/m^2/h$ at ambient temperatures of 45° C. Even when dehydrated, waterbuck are unable to reduce their water loss. This lack of ability to reduce both respiratory and cutaneous water loss explains the very restricted niche occupied by waterbuck in dry areas.

Oryx are well adapted to desert conditions because of their ability to change the method by which they dissipate water according to their state of hydration. When fully hydrated, the rate of sweating starts to rise from a basal level well below $50gH_2O/m^2/h$ at 30° C ambient temperature to a level approaching $150 gH_2O/m^2/h$ at 45° C (Fig. 4.13). When dehydrated, oryx no longer sweated even when the ambient temperature reached 46° C, this being due in large part to the manner in which oryx allow their core temperature to rise in response to high ambient temperatures.

The hartebeest, wildebeest and impala all have very low rates of sweating which increase only slightly even under very high environmental heat loads. Evaporative water loss in the hartebeest starts very suddenly at skin temperatures of between 33° C and 36° C, as it does in the eland (Finch 1972a). In the hartebeest, however, unlike the eland, it is only the respiration rate that is affected by the heat load: the sweating rate, which is extremely low at temperatures of 20° C, does not exceed $60gH_2O/m^2/h$ at 50° C. Also unlike the eland, the skin temperature of the hartebeest exceeds rectal temperature when this reaches about 39° C, and there is therefore a net heat flow into the body. The hartebeest is able to dissipate this influx of heat plus some metabolic heat via the respiratory route (Finch 1972a).

At low temperatures of 22° C in a climate chamber, both hartebeest and impala evaporate almost half of their water via the cutaneous route: when dehydrated, both species lose most water by an increase in the rate of respiration. Impala had a lower sweating rate, about $50gH_2O/m^2/h$, than hartebeest at 50° C (Maloiy and Hopcraft 1971). Neither increases in temperature nor changes in the state of hydration had any effect on sweating by wildebeest. The basal rate of sweating of about $50gH_2O/m^2/h$ at 20° C was maintained under all conditions (Taylor 1970b).

With the exception of the Dorcas, medium- and small-sized gazelle have relatively low rates of water loss by sweating. The sweat rate remains within a few grams of $50gH_2O/m^2/h$ in both Grant's and Thomson's gazelles at low and high ambient temperatures and whether or not the animals are dehydrated (Taylor 1970b). Sweating contributes very little to heat dissipation in either Grant's or Thomson's gazelle (Taylor 1972). Gazelle show a synchronous periodic discharge of sweat somewhat similar to that of domestic small ruminants and oryx (Robertshaw and Taylor 1969).

The dik-dik is not a ruminant that sweats actively and has a density of sweat glands of about $190/cm^2$, similar to that found in camels, goats and sheep, but much less than that in cattle. The low density of sweat glands must, in part, be responsible for the low level of sweating which does not exceed $19gH_2O/m^2/h$, which is equivalent to a maximum of $6gH_2O/h$ over the whole body surface. Increases in the sweating rate can be induced by injections of adrenalin but not by noradrenalin (Maloiy 1973a) and it thus appears that the sweat glands of dik-dik are under adrenergic-neurone control as in other ruminants.

4.4.3   Faeces

When ample water is available and animals are not dehydrated, considerable amounts of water are excreted with the faeces. Water loss in faeces is not expressed in the normal way as a percentage of the total volume but as $gH_2O/100g$ faecal dry matter. This method of expression is used because the percentage digestibility of a food determines the amount of dry matter that passes through the gastro-intestinal tract. If, therefore, the amount of water that is lost with each unit of undigested dry matter is known, it is relatively easy to calculate the total water loss.

The total amount of faeces and their water content vary, then, according to the type of food and its digestibility. Ruminants are able to extract considerable amounts of water from the intestinal contents, and this process is very much more efficient in arid-adapted animals when dehydrated. All the major species of domestic ruminants have been shown to be able to reabsorb a greater proportion of gastro-intestinal water when dehydrated while at the same time increasing the concentration of electrolytes in the retained fluid (Maloiy, Taylor and Clemens 1978).

Reduction of the amount of water in the faeces is achieved by sodium absorption in the colon, accompanied by a return of water to the blood. The overall response to dehydration in both domestic and wild ruminants is a reduction of between 10 and 35% of faecal water (Table 4.9) while the total amount of electrolytes in the gut is not seriously affected. In most ruminants the loss of water in the faeces represents a considerably lesser proportion of the total water loss than does evaporative water loss. Faeces with low water content are characteristically formed as pellets, and even the usually large cakes of dung produced by cattle occasionally assume this form under conditions of severe dehydration.

Table 4.9. Faecal water content of desert and non-desert ruminants when fully watered and when dehydrated (temperature regime in climatic chamber at 22°C/40°C except where noted)

Species	Water content (g H_2O/100 g dry matter)			Source
	Animals fully watered	Animals dehydrated	Per cent decrease	
Camel[a]	109	76	30	Schmidt-Nielsen et al. (1956)
Camel[a]	268	168	38	Charnot (1958)
Temperate cattle	362	302	17	Taylor and Lyman (1967)
Goat[b]	140	88	37	Schoen (1968)
Goat	132	106	20	Maloiy and Taylor (1971)
Sheep	134	93	31	Maloiy and Taylor (1971)
Eland	195	160	18	Taylor and Lyman (1967)
Waterbuck[c]	270	212	21	Taylor, Spinage and Lyman (1969)
Hartebeest	138	108	22	Maloiy and Hopcraft (1971)
Impala	142	114	20	Maloiy and Hopcraft (1971)
Dorcas gazelle[d]	113	75	34	Ghobrial (1974)

[a] Natural conditions

[b] Temperature 18°C/30°

[c] 22°

[d] Winter and summer conditions, average temperatures max/min 50–55°C/25–35°C in summer and 30–40°C/15–25°C in winter

Camels excrete the driest faeces of all domestic ruminants and, of all ruminants so far studied, are second only to the dik-dik in the small amount of water excreted by the faecal route (Table 4.9). In a climatic chamber at 22° C, fully hydrated camels lost about 30% of the total water they used in the faeces, this being equivalent to about 0.6 litres/100 kg/day. When deprived of water, at 22° C the proportion of faecal to total water loss was about the same but the actual use of water in the faeces was reduced to about 0.3 litres/100kg/day (Maloiy 1972c). Under a periodic heat load of 12 hours at 22° C and 12 hours at 40° C, the contribution of faecal water loss to total water loss in hydrated camels was only about 16%: the actual loss in this state was similar to that in hydrated camels at a constant 22° C, the lowered proportion being due to a large increase in evaporative water use. In dehydrated camels at 22° C/40° C, faecal water loss was reduced to about 0.25 litres/100kg/day and its contribution to total water use was reduced to about 13%. In these climatic chamber experiments much of the reduction in faecal water loss was due to a reduced food intake, which was down by about 32% in dehydrated compared to hydrated camels at the alternating low and high temperature treatment (Maloiy 1972c). It should be remembered, however, that under natural conditions the camel does not lose its appetite when dehydrated, as it selects the more succulent vegetation. In the natural situation, therefore, faecal water loss would most probably be higher than in the climatic chamber.

About 33% of total water use in temperate steers under temperate conditions is via the faeces. Total water loss in faeces averaged about 1.92 litres/100kg/day at 22° C when fully hydrated, this being reduced to 1.51 litres after dehydration (Taylor and Lyman 1967). At high temperatures (22° C/40° C), water in the faeces of hydrated animals was similar to that at the low-temperature regime (1.99 litres/100kg/day), but dehydrated animals were not able to reduce this and still maintained a fairly high output of faecal water (1.87 litres/100kg/day).

Arid-adapted goats and sheep in Kenya lost a much smaller proportion of total water via the faeces than did cattle. At 22° C in the climatic chamber both Turkana goats and fat-tailed sheep lost about 20% of water via the faeces when they were fully hydrated (about 1.3 litres/100kg/day and 1.0 litres/100kg/day respectively), but under conditions of restricted water the loss was reduced by 61% in goats and by 57% in sheep (Maloiy and Taylor 1971). Only half of the reduction was explained by drier faeces (Table 4.9), the remainder of the reduction being due to a lower food intake. When a heat load was applied and water was available ad libitum, sheep increased water loss in the faeces by 43%, mainly due to a higher food intake. In heat-loaded goats with water freely available, faecal water loss was reduced by 45%, this being mainly due to a lowered food intake. Dehydrated and heat-stressed animals of both species showed reactions that were similar to those when they were not heat-stressed.

Bedouin goats in the Sinai desert of Israel probably lose a slightly lesser proportion of water via the faeces than do East African small ruminants. In normally watered goats the loss of water via the faeces was less than 18% of total water loss. The faecal water content was also less than in East African goats, being about $100gH_2O/100g$ faecal dry matter in fully watered goats (50% water content), but only about $65gH_2O/100g$ faecal dry matter to $70gH_2O/100g$ faecal dry matter (40% water content) in goats deprived of water (Shkolnik, Borut and Choshniak 1972). The reduction in water content was equivalent to 30 to 35%, this being within the normal range found in other ruminants.

Faecal water loss in the eland varies between 20% (Taylor 1969a) and 33% (Taylor and Lyman 1967) of total water loss. Eland had a faecal water output of 1.74 litres/100kg/day when fully watered at 22° C, this dropping to 1.54 litres/100 kg/day when the animals were deprived of water. At alternating low and high temperatures of 22° C and 40° C, in contrast to the temperate type steers in the same experiment, faecal water loss by the eland was reduced to 1.50 litres/100kg/day in fully watered animals and was reduced even further to 1.19 litres/100kg/day in dehydrated animals. The similarity of total faecal water loss per 100kg live weight by both species at the low temperature is explained by the higher metabolic rate of eland in comparison to cattle. In cool conditions the eland consumes more than 30% more oxygen than cattle. The higher food consumption of the eland (1.67% of body weight) compared to the temperate steer (1.33% of body weight) and the difference in digestibility (52% for the eland and 58% for cattle) explain the similarities in total faecal water produced (Taylor and Lyman 1967).

At temperatures of 22° C, fully hydrated waterbuck lost about one-third of their total water via the faeces, equivalent to about 2.0 litres/100kg/day. When dehydrated the amount of water in the faeces was reduced by about 21% (Table 4.9). Total faecal water was reduced to about half its original level due, in part, to a lowered food intake which dropped from 1.90% of live weight with water ad libitum to 1.61% of live weight when water was restricted. In waterbuck with free access to water but subjected to alternating temperatures of 22° C and 40° C for 12 hours each, water loss in the faeces did not increase, but its contribution to total water use dropped to about 16% as there was a large increase in evaporative water demand and some increase in urine flow (Taylor, Spinage and Lyman 1969).

The contribution of faecal water to total water loss in the oryx is rather small and amounts to about 16% (Taylor 1969a). The level is higher both in hartebeest, in which it is about 23%, and in impala, where it is about 26% (Maloiy and Hopcraft 1971) in fully hydrated animals at 22° C. Under these non-stressful conditions, total faecal water loss was about 1.3 litres/100kg/day in hartebeest and 1.2 litres/100kg/day in impala. When water was restricted at 22° C the contribution of faecal water to total water loss increased slightly in both hartebeest and impala, indicating that greater savings were being made in evaporative loss. The total volume of faecal water was still reduced, however, to about 0.78 litres/100kg/day both in hartebeest and in impala, the smaller quantity being in part due to a lowered food consumption and in part to the lower water intake. At alternating temperatures of 22° C and 40° C hartebeest reduced total faecal water output considerably even when provided with water ad libitum (0.63 litres/100kg/day), while impala reduced their output to a lesser degree (1.00 litres/100kg/day). When both heat stress and a restricted water regime were applied, faecal water output was considerably reduced in both hartebeest (0.47 litres/100kg/day) and impala (0.69 litres/100kg/day) (Maloiy and Hopcraft 1971).

In Dorcas gazelle, which have a faecal water content similar to that of the camel (Table 4.9), faecal water loss in animals in winter was equivalent to 0.34 litres/100 kg/day, this dropping to 0.09 litres/100 kg/day in dehydrated gazelle. In summer, hydrated gazelle excreted 0.16 litres/100kg/day in their faeces, but reduced this to 0.05 litres/100kg/day when deprived of water (Ghobrial 1974).

Dik-dik excrete the driest faeces of all desert ruminants studied (Table 4.9). In contrast to most other ruminants, the dik-dik has an increased faecal water output at higher temperatures whether it has access to water or not, this probably being due to a higher feed intake. At both constant low and alternating low/high temperatures, faecal water output was reduced in the dehydrated compared to the hydrated state. Total faecal water output at 22° C in hydrated dik-dik averaged 50.7 g for four animals and for dehydrated animals averaged 37.5g. Assuming an average weight of 4kg (Maloiy 1973a), this is equivalent to 1.27 litres/100kg/day and 0.94 litres/100kg/day respectively. At 22° C/40° C hydrated animals passed an average of 64.5g of water in the faeces, while dehydrated ones excreted 43.5g, these being equivalent, respectively, to 1.61 litres/100kg/day and 1.09 litres/100kg/day. The dik-dik is able to save between 10g and 20g of water per day by excreting drier faeces, this being rather less than the 20 to 40g of water it conserves by concentrating its urine and the 70 to 100g it saves by decreased evaporation (Maloiy 1973a).

4.4.4   Urine and Kidney Function

The ability of the mammalian kidney to concentrate urine is considered to be an important factor contributing to survival in arid lands. Many ruminant kidneys are able to concentrate urine to a considerable degree. As for conservation of water by the faeces, the two most efficient ruminants appear to be the camel (Maloiy 1972c) and the dik-dik (Schoen 1969). The ruminant kidney fails, however, to reach the concentrating power of small rodents. The main reason for this is probably because even very concentrated urine, which can then be voided in small amounts, results in only minor savings in total water loss in ruminants, which have greater requirements for water for evaporative cooling. In small rodents, an efficient renal mechanism is literally vital, as their whole water balance depends on the kidney's ability to conserve water. The amount of water used by the mammalian kidney is dependent on the amount of waste products that have to be eliminated but, as a major end-product of metabolism is urea and as this is voided in solution, a certain minimal amount of water is required. Birds, reptiles and insects excrete most of the end-products of nitrogen metabolism as insoluble uric acid and therefore need little or no water in its evacuation.

Reductions in the glomerular filtration rate and in renal plasma flow are responsible for the reduced urine flow and the reduced kidney function is more pronounced in dehydrated than in hydrated animals. The loops of Henle in the nephron of the mammalian kidney are the main site at which water loss in the urine can be minimised and they are responsible for the production of urine which is hypotonic to the plasma. Some examples of the ability to concentrate urine in relation to plasma concentration in terms of total osmolarity are provided in Table 4.10. As just stated, the main site of concentration of urine is the loops of Henle: the more long loops of Henle there are, the greater the concentrating ability. Among domestic animals, camels and sheep have more long loops than cattle.

The ratio of the thickness of the medulla to that of the cortex provides a good index of the potential to reabsorb water and produce a concentrated urine (Schmidt-Nielsen and O'Dell 1961). Desert mammals such as the kangaroo rat have a relative medullary thickness of 8.5 and a maximal urinary:plasma ratio of 14.0:1.0, while non-desert mammals such as man have a relative medullary thickness of 3.0 and a maximum urine:plasma ratio of 4.2:1.0. In the pig, primarily a forest species, the relative medullary thickness is only 1.6 (Schmidt-Nielsen and O'Dell 1961). In semi-arid species such as the springbok and the bontebok (*Damaliscus dorcas*), medullary thicknesses

Table 4.10. Maximum ratios of urinary to plasma concentrations for different ruminants

Species	Urinary: plasma ratio	Source
Camel	8.0	Maloiy (1972c)
Temperate cattle	4.0	Taylor and Lyman (1967)
Zebu steer	4.0	Maloiy (1972c)
Bedouin goat	7.0	Maloiy, Macfarlane and Shkolnik (1979)
Eland	6.0	Taylor and Lyman (1967)
Waterbuck	4.0	Taylor, Spinage and Lyman (1969)
Springbok	7.0	Hofmeyr and Louw (1987)
Bontebok	5.4	Hofmeyr and Louw (1987)
Grant's gazelle	8.0	Maloiy, Macfarlane and Shkolnik (1979)
Dik-dik	11.0	Maloiy (1973a)

Table 4.11. Total urine volume in ruminants when hydrated and when dehydrated

Species	Urine volume (litres/100 kg live weight/day)		% Change	Source
	Hydrated	Dehydrated		
Camel[a]	0.29	0.07	76	Maloiy (1972c)
Temperate steer	0.98	0.72	27	Taylor and Lyman (1967)
East African goat	0.70	0.40	43	Maloiy and Taylor (1971)
Barmer goat (India)[b]	2.52	0.61	76	Khan, Ghosh and Sasidharan (1978)
Bedouin goat[c]	1.71	—	—	Shkolnik, Borut and Chosniak (1972)
East African sheep	0.80	0.20	75	Maloiy and Taylor (1971)
Marwari sheep (India)[d]	1.49	0.73	51	Ghosh, Khan and Abichandani (1976)
Eland	1.57	0.73	54	Taylor and Lyman (1967)
Waterbuck[e]	2.70	2.70	0	Taylor, Spinage and Lyman (1969)
Hartebeest	0.72	0.42	42	Maloiy and Hopcraft (1971)
Impala	1.24	0.32	74	Maloiy and Hopcraft (1971)
Dorcas gazelle[f]	2.10	1.40	33	Ghobrial (1970a)
Dik-dik[g]	2.03	1.01	50	Maloiy (1973a)

[a] Calculated from the original data of 857 ml and 205 ml for hydrated and dehydrated camels at an alternating 12-hour temperature regime of 22°C and 40°C. All data relate to these conditions except where otherwise noted
[b] Maximum temperature ≈ 36°C, minimum 17°C under covered verandah
[c] Constant 30°C
[d] Maximum temperature ≈ 38°C, minimum 24°C inside canvas canopy
[e] Constant 22°C
[f] "Hydrated" = winter, maximum temperature 30°C–40°C; "dehydrated" = summer, maximum temperature 50°C–55°C
[g] Caluclated from original data of 81.5 ml/day and 40.5 ml/day

are 5.3 and 4.9 respectively (Hofmeyr and Louw 1987). The relative volume of the medulla to that of the whole kidney has also been used as an indication of adaptation to aridity (Schoen 1969) and is higher in dik-dik (47 %) than in the Uganda kob (*Adenota kob*) of the semi-arid zone (38%) and the bushbuck (*Tragelaphus scriptus*) of sub-humid woodland (31%).

When subject to dehydration, arid-adapted ruminants reduce the volume of their urine (Table 4.11) but increase its concentration (Table 4.12). In general, the increase in osmolarity results from increases in sodium levels as well as in the concentration of urea. Potassium and chloride levels are affected to a lesser degree. There are exceptions to these general statements. Kidney function is under the control of ADH (vasopressin) and aldosterone.

Table 4.12. Urine osmolarity in hydrated and dehydrated ruminants

Species	Osmolarity (mOsm/litre)		% Change	Source
	Hydrated	Dehydrated		
Camel[a]	1473	2230	51	Maloiy (1972c)
Camel[b]	620	2100	239	Etzion and Yagil (1986)
Temperate steer	855	1043	22	Taylor and Lyman (1967)
East African goat[c]	895	1425	59	Schoen (1968)
Bedouin goat[d]	1315	1771	35	Chosniak et al. (1984)
Eland	637	1881	195	Taylor and Lyman (1967)
Waterbuck[e]	1060	1090	3	Taylor, Spinage and Lyman (1969)
Hartebeest	1128	2010	78	Maloiy and Hopcraft (1971)
Impala	1410	2250	60	Maloiy and Hopcraft (1971)
Dorcas gazelle[f]	1200	2300	92	Ghobrial (1974)
Springbok[g]	1251	—	—	Hofmeyr and Louw (1987)
Dik-dik	1814	3907	115	Maloiy (1973a)
Dik-dik	2235	4762	113	Schoen (1969)
Bushbuck	936	1345	44	Schoen (1969)
Uganda kob	1109	1594	44	Schoen (1969)

[a] At periodic heat of 22°C and 40°C for 12 hours each. All other data relate to these conditions except where stated otherwise
[b] Free ranging animals in shaded yard at 38°C: hydrated = 2 hours after drinking
[c] At periodic heat of 18°C and 30°C
[d] Free ranging under traditional management: dehydrated = 4 days without water; hydrated = 3–4 hours after drinking
[e] Constant 22°C
[f] "Summer" maximum temperature 50°C–55°C, minimum 25°C–35°C
[g] Animals shot in the field: based on relative medullary thickness maximum concentration would be 2700–3000 mOsm

The camel is undoubtedly the most celebrated of desert ruminants for its ability to withstand heat and aridity. This ability results from the particular physiological characteristics of the camel which are: a tolerance of extreme dehydration while continuing to maintain major body functions at a more or less normal level; an ability to reduce overall water use; a reduction in faecal water content; and a greatly reduced urine flow with a high concentration of solutes.

The normally low volumes of urine voided by the camel are reduced even further under dehydration (Table 4.11) and a relatively high total osmolarity is further increased (Table 4.12). In relation to its body weight, the camel passes very little urine even when it has free access to water and the total amount rarely exceeds 5 litres/day. In addition to voiding a small amount in total, the camel has another peculiarity which consists of frequent urinations, each of very small volume (indicating that the camel bladder is very small), which are also passed in a peculiar manner. The male has a fold in the prepuce which causes it to urinate, like the female, towards the rear: in both sexes a rhythmic release of the sphincter causes the urine to be emptied in a series of small jets and the whole process takes a considerable time. The habit that the camel has of urinating on its legs has been construed as an additional adaptation to the desert, as it does cause some evaporative cooling.

Maximal urinary osmolar concentrations in the camel are reported to be even higher than shown in Table 4.12 and may reach 3100mOsm/litre. Following dehydration, urea accounts for a large proportion of the increased osmolarity, being more than 50% higher (954mM/litre) in camels dehydrated at 22° C/40° C than in fully watered camels (618mM/litre) in the same environmental conditions (Maloiy 1972c). There are also considerable increases in urinary sodium levels and in potassium and chloride, although the proportional rise in the last two is less than it is in sodium.

The total excreted amount of sodium and potassium might, however, be reduced because of the reduced urine volume. Plasma electrolyte levels also rise but to a much lesser extent (Fig. 4.14). At the same time there is a reduction in the glomerular filtration rate, which declines by about 30% from 179ml/min to 124ml/min. In the dehydrated animals, renal tubular absorption

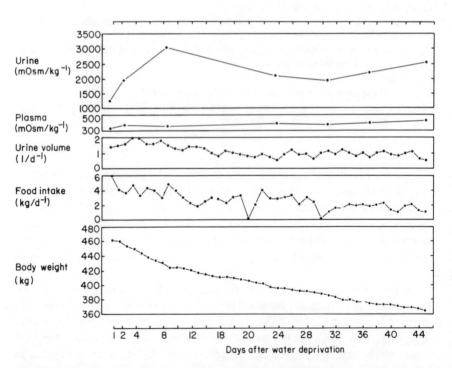

Fig. 4.14. Changes in urine and plasma osmolarities, in urine volume and in food intake and weight in a camel deprived of water for 45 days at 22°C (Maloiy 1972 c)

of water from the glomerular filtrate is almost 100 per cent. When rehydrated with NaCl solutions of higher concentration than sea water, fluid intake is greater than when drinking fresh water. Camels drinking salt solution produce a greater volume of urine than watered camels, have greatly elevated levels of sodium and chloride but reduced levels of potassium in the urine, a higher total osmolarity and increased glomerular filtration and urine flow rates (Maloiy 1972c).

A number of other studies have shown the depressed function of the camel kidney under dehydration (Siebert and Macfarlane 1971; Yagil and Berlyne 1978b), including a much greater reduction in glomerular filtration rate from about 60ml/100kg/min to 15ml/100kg/min (Macfarlane 1968). In Israel, glomerular filtration rates were also reduced by about 75% from 0.81ml/kg/min to 0.23ml/kg/min, this being accompanied by a similar reduction in renal plasma flow (Yagil and Berlyne 1978b) but by increased concentrations of ADH and aldosterone (Yagil and Etzion 1979).

The kidney of camels probably responds to ADH in reducing the glomerular filtration rate but other mechanisms, including circulatory ones, are probably also involved. ADH injected intravenously into camels (Fig. 4.15) can reduce urine flow from 5ml/min to 3ml/min in animals with excess water, while at the same time increasing the levels of potassium (Macfarlane 1968). In camels with a normal or low urine flow, injection of larger amounts of ADH increases both potassium and chloride excretion (and possibly also sodium excretion) and these electrolytes result in a temporary increase of urine flow in order that they may be transported.

When camels are allowed to drink immediately to satiation the kidney function rapidly returns to normal (Etzion and Yagil 1986). Within half an hour there is a significant increase in the urine flow rate, in glomerular filtration rate and in renal plasma flow, while there are significant decreases

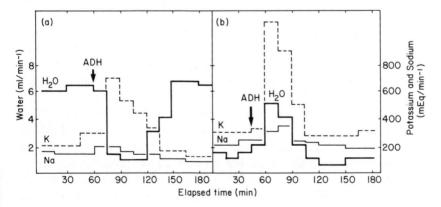

Fig. 4.15. Effects of vasopressin injections on water and electrolytes in *(a)* water loaded and *(b)* normal camels (Macfarlane 1968)

in plasma and urine osmolarities and in the osmolar clearance rate. Urine urea, urea clearances and filtered urea all increased significantly within two hours of drinking, these probably being associated with a reduction in ADH levels.

Both temperate and tropical types of cattle are less efficient at concentrating urine than camels or the domestic small ruminants. The maximum urinary:plasma osmolar ratio achievable by cattle is about 4:1 (Table 4.10), while urine volume can be reduced by less than 30% and osmolarity increased by only just over 20% (Tables 4.11, 4.12). Cattle are much less sensitive to the effects of ADH, in respect of both its antidiuretic effects and its effects on potassium output, than are sheep. Effective doses of ADH for increasing potassium output are about 110g/kg for cattle compared to 20g/kg for sheep and for decreasing urine flow they are 30g/kg and 3g/kg respectively (Macfarlane 1964). Cattle do respond to low dietary quantity and poor quality, however, in much the same way as camels and small ruminants by reabsorbing urea for recirculation in the saliva and across the rumen wall (Livingston, Payne and Friend 1964).

Goats and sheep have the ability to achieve urinary:plasma osmolar ratios in the range of 6:1 to 8:1 (Table 4.10, Maloiy 1973b). Urine volumes can be reduced, depending on the breed or type of animal, by from 50% to almost 80% when under water stress (Table 4.11). Urine osmolarity is increased by from 35% to 60% concomitant on reduced urine flow (Table 4.12).

In Barmer goats in the Rajasthan desert the glomerular filtration rate has been reported to be reduced to one-third of its normal value when animals are severely dehydrated: the GFR decreased from a mean of 49.5ml/min to one of 16.9ml/min (Khan, Sasidharan and Ghosh 1979). Although there was a sharp increase in blood urea in these Barmer goats, there was no decrease in the concentration of urinary urea following dehydration, but a reduction in urine flow to less than 25% of the original after 4 days (Khan, Ghosh and Sasidharan 1978) means that total urea excretion was greatly reduced. Marwari sheep in the same environment as the Barmer goats had a glomerular filtration rate that was reduced to about 20% of the initial value after 2 days of water deprivation (Ghosh, Khan and Abichandani 1976): urine volume was reduced to about 43% of the initial value, while urine electrolytes increased by more than 30%, the higher concentration being achieved mainly by an increase in sodium levels.

In East African goats and sheep, urinary water loss was only about 10 to 15% of total water loss in experimental animals when freely watered (Maloiy and Taylor 1971). An increased periodic heat load in these species when fully hydrated did not affect urine output but, when water was restricted in addition, the volume of urine fell to less than 50% of that produced by watered animals. Other experiments on East African goats have shown savings of water in the urine of a similar magnitude, while the increase in osmolarity was of the order of 60% (Schoen 1968). Total cation excretion was reduced in spite of higher concentrations in the urine because of the reduced urine volume, and this appears to confirm that there is hormonal control of potassium excretion to allow maximal excretion of the waste products of metabolism under water stress.

In Bedouin goats in the Negev, urine flow rates dropped lower after rapid rehydration than they were in dehydrated animals (Choshniak et al. 1984). It is suggested that the rate of flow of the renal plasma is the major factor in controlling this drop, as both urine flow and glomerular filtration rates follow the changes in the renal plasma flow. It is further suggested that the reduction in kidney function is caused by the excitement of the animal at the sight of water, as similar excitement stimuli have been reported for camels (Finberg, Yagil and Berlyne 1978), for cattle (Bianca 1970), and elsewhere for goats (Maltz et al. 1984).

Many desert-adapted wild ruminants have the ability to reduce urine flow and concentrate electrolytes in the urine to a high degree. Most of these animals, as might be expected, have very wide ratios of urinary:plasma osmolarities ranging from 6:1 in the eland to about 11:1 in the dik-dik (Table 4.10). Reduction in urine volume varies from a rather surprisingly low amount of 33% in the Dorcas gazelle to one of 74% in the impala (Table 4.11). Increases in osmolarity vary from 60% in the impala to 195% in the eland. Non-adapted antelopes living in restricted niches in the arid zones have much less efficient urinary response mechanisms to water deprivation. The waterbuck, for example, has a maximum urinary:plasma osmolar ratio of 4:1, can reduce its urine volume hardly at all and is incapable of producing a more concentrated urine (Taylor, Spinage and Lyman 1969).

Under experimental conditions, a thermal load did not reduce the volume of urine produced by eland when water was available ad libitum but there were 50% and 70% decreases in potassium and chloride, accompanied by a decrease in osmotic pressure (Taylor and Lyman 1967). A higher loss of these two ions through sweating was possibly responsible for the decrease. When water was restricted, urine volume was reduced to one-half or one-third of that in fully hydrated animals. At high temperatures and restricted water, the eland reabsorbed almost all its sodium intake but excreted considerable amounts of potassium, and high urine osmolarity was achieved principally by excreting fairly large amounts of urea. Under field conditions, urea contributed 25 to 40% of total urine osmolarity, these large amounts presumably being due to the ability of the eland to select a diet high in protein as a result of its browsing habits. Hartebeest and impala both double urine osmolarity when dehydrated and both species concentrate sodium, potassium, chloride and urea (Maloiy and Hopcraft 1971).

In winter, when provided free access to water, Dorcas gazelle had a daily output of 347ml of urine with a specific gravity of 1.038, the volume being equivalent to about 2.1% of body weight. The osmolar concentration in winter was about 1400mOsm/litre. Under hot summer conditions the output of urine dropped to about 200ml (1.4% of body weight) but there were no changes in specific gravity (1.028) or in osmolarity (1200mOsm/litre). When deprived of water, there was a reduction in urine volume to about one-third or one-quarter of that excreted by the fully watered animal and osmolarity increased to 2300mOsm/l. The concentrated urine had 70% more urea and 52% more potassium than the dilute form, but there was a decrease of 25% in sodium and 26% in chloride. The reduction in urinary chloride was again considered to be due to greater losses through sweating (Ghobrial 1970a, 1974).

Dik-dik are able to concentrate their urine so that the urine:plasma osmolar ratio is as high as 11:1 (Maloiy 1973a) or even 15:1 (Schoen 1972). Dik-dik therefore can conserve considerable amounts of water by excreting the waste products of metabolism in a very concentrated form. Sodium concentrations in the urine were reduced in heat-stressed and water-deprived dik-dik, while potassium and chloride concentrations were increased. As the dik-dik pants rather than sweats to reduce heat load, chloride would not be lost in cutaneous evaporation. Urea concentrations also increased greatly as a reault of the reduction in urine volume. Although potassium was the principal ion excreted under all experimental conditions, there was a small decrease in potassium excretion when dik-dik were dehydrated. Conversely, urea excretion was considerably increased in conditions of both heat with ad libitum water and heat with restricted water (Maloiy 1973a).

4.4.5   Lactation

Milk production imposes extra demands on water economy under any condition, but these demands can be relatively very high in arid zones. Water consumed by lactating Bedouin goats has been shown to be about three times that consumed in dry goats (Maltz and Shkolnik 1980). Water turnover in these goats was more than twice as much in lactating females compared to non-lactating ones. Although water output in milk was only about 61ml/kg/day, output of water by the evaporative, faecal and urinary routes was also higher in lactating goats than in dry ones, presumably due to the additional stress caused by the production of milk. The water lost through milk exceeded that lost in faeces and urine combined and was about two-thirds of that lost by evaporation. The average milk production of 1.8kg/female/day to 2.0kg/female/day was equivalent to about 8 or 9% of body weight.

During lactation the goats gained weight, this being largely due to an increased body water (HTO) space, which could be 35% greater than in non-lactating goats (Maltz and Shkolnik 1980). Body water space was reduced during the course of dehydration, but was regained following drinking. Milk yield was also reduced consequent on dehydration but increased again following intake of water. Constant hydration-dehydration cycles had no effect on the ability of the goat to maintain the recovery of milk production at its initial level. The EB space closely reflected the changes in HTO space. The Bedouin goat seems adapted to desert conditions by being able to expand its water-storing capacity during lactation and to make use of this excess to produce milk and to sustain itself over relatively long periods of water deprivation.

Another adaptation to desert conditions is the ability of the camel to dilute its milk. This dilution involves the production of milk with a higher water content when the animal is dehydrated than when it is fully watered (Yagil and Etzion 1980). The ability to dilute milk under similar conditions of water stress has also been demonstrated in the human female and in cattle (Yagil et al. 1986). Milk dilution is not reported for other mammals. Dilution involves a reduction of fat, lactose, protein, calcium and magnesium but an increase in sodium, phosphorus, phosphate and chloride, with no changes in urea levels. It was considered that the dilution of milk under dehydration was a physiological adaptation to ensure an adequate supply of water to young animals with access to no other source, while at the same time continuing to provide them with an adequate supply of other nutrients. It was also postulated that the hormones governing milk production and secretion – prolactin and oxytocin – act in a manner similar to and, indeed, in conjunction with the hormones responsible for water homeostasis. Prolactin and oxytocin thus reinforce the effects of ADH and aldosterone in causing water to be withdrawn from the store in the intestines and secreting it into the milk (Yagil et al. 1986).

5 Nutrition

5.1 Introduction

Mammals have developed a wide spectrum of nutritional as well as ecophysiological adaptations to very diverse habitats and a range of different types of food. In herbivorous mammals, two major sites of digestion and fermentation of the ingested food have become clearly differentiated. These sites are the forestomach and the hindgut. Forestomach fermenters are essentially adapted to low-quality food. This is because it is of advantage to break low-quality food down into its digestible components as early in the process as possible. Hindgut fermenters adapted to a high-quality diet have less need for such an early breakdown of food. Forestomach fermenters can therefore be considered

Table 5.1. A classification of arid-zone ruminants according rating and preferred types of food

Herbivory class	Preferred food	Examples
1. Omnivores	Animal material (55%), fruits tubers, occasional buds and shoots (45%)	(Hindgut fermenters only)
2. Concentrate selectors	Fruits, tubers, seeds, flowers (65%); leaves (10%); (occassional animal material, 25%)	(Some non-ruminantia among forestomach fermenters)
3. Concentrate selectors	Leaves of leguminosae and other plants (35%); seeds, blossoms, young shoots (65%)	Goat, camel, dik-dik, steenbok, gerenuk, kudu, giraffe
4. Intermediate feeders	Leaves, shoots, fruits and blossoms (65%); tubers, seeds and other reserve organs (35%)	Sheep, impala, Grant's gazelle, eland, springbok
5. Bulk and roughage feeders	Mainly leaves, shoots and plant stems (60%); a good proportion of grass (40%)	Thomson's gazelle, hartebeest, oryx, gemsbok
6. Bulk and roughage feeders	Grass (100%)	Cattle, buffalo, wildebeest

to be more likely to be found in open biomes (Langer 1984). Desert ruminants are forestomach fermenters adapted to poor-quality food in open biomes. They are also usually adapted to periodic nutritional stress which they combat through a series of different strategies, including deposition of fat, reduction of metabolic rate and, in extreme cases, migration. Non-ruminant herbivores and non-herbivorous animals have adopted these and other strategies.

Within the guild of herbivores, including both forestomach and hindgut types, three major groups of animals have been proposed according to the type of food they prefer (Hofmann and Stewart 1972; Hofmann 1973). This typology has subsequently been refined into six classes (Langer 1984) based on food preferences and, in some cases, on the relative amounts of different food components in the overall diet. The typology of these classes, the food preferred and an assignment of domestic and wild desert ruminants within the classes is provided in Table 5.1. It should be noted that the classification of Table 5.1 ignores or overrides the distinction that is commonly used between grazers and browsers and is based on feeding habits and stomach structure.

5.2   Structure and Function of the Digestive System of the Camelidae

5.2.1   The Buccal Cavity

All Camelidae have a thin upper lip which is split in the middle and is more or less prehensile. These characteristics are well marked in the dromedary (Fig. 5.1). The lower lip is larger and pendulous. The upper dental pad is hard and horn-like. Papillae on the inner cheek point backwards, towards the throat. The hard palate is long and the soft palate is often extruded from the mouth, particularly by male *Camelus* in rut. The small tongue is very mobile and is furnished with five to seven large papillae on each side. Dentition

Fig. 5.1. The prehensile upper lip of a one-humped camel selecting leaves of *Leptadenia hastata* in central Mali

differs from that of true or advanced ruminants: there are incisors in the upper jaw and both upper and lower jaws have canine teeth or "tushes". Dental differences from true ruminants are less marked in the South American camelids.

The salivary glands are similar anatomically to those of other ruminating animals. Their function also seems to be similar, and secretory rates and composition of saliva also closely resemble those of advanced ruminants (von Engelhardt and Sallman 1972). There is some evidence, at least in alpaca (*Lama pacos*), that salivary flow might be greater in Camelidae than in Ruminantia.

5.2.2   Pharynx and Oesophagus

The pharynx is partly divided into two compartments by a constriction of the long, narrow tube which forms it. The oesophagus is of large capacity, about 1 to 2 metres long, and has secreting glands which apparently assist the salivary glands to moisturize the food.

5.2.3   Stomach

The camelid stomach differs from that of the Ruminantia in a number of respects. There are only three distinct compartments in the camelid stomach

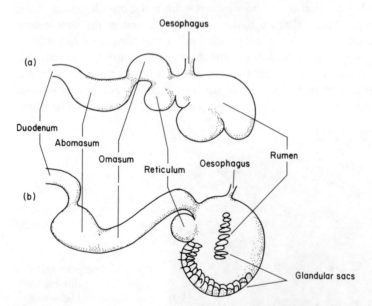

Fig. 5.2. A schematic comparison of the stomach anatomy of *(a)* Ruminantia and *(b)* Tylopoda

compared to four in advanced ruminants (Fig. 5.2). While it has been conventional to refer to the different parts of the camelid stomach by the same terminology as that used for ruminants, it is not certain that the parts which perform analogous functions are homologous. It is therefore perhaps preferable to refer to the separate parts as compartments. The rumen thus becomes C1 and this can be divided into cranial and caudal sacs. The second, much smaller compartment, the reticulum, is nominated C2. This has a ventricular groove, which apparently has a function similar to the reticular groove of the Ruminantia. The ventricular groove terminates at the entrance to the elongated C3 or combined omasum/abomasum.

The rumen and reticulum (C1 and C2) are also referred to as the forestomach. The "glandular sac" areas of the camelid stomach were once considered to be the water store of the animal. The sacs consist of a number of small chambers separated by folds of mucosa which are covered by a columnar epithelium in the dorsal (cranial) part of C1 and by glands in the ventral (caudal) part. The mucosal areas probably function as absorption and fermentation areas as well as zones of enzymatic secretion.

As already noted, there is no sharp distinction between omasum and abomasum in camelids and this might best be referred to as the tubular stomach: its terminal part is only one-fifth of the total length, is very thick and is the site of the gastric glands (von Engelhardt and Heller 1985).

5.2.4   Intestines

In a full-grown dromedary the small intestine can be as long as 40 metres. A common duct from the pancreas and the liver opens into the looped duodenum. The abomasum, or distal end of the tubular stomach, is largely occupied by the jejunum along which there is a chain of mesenteric lymph nodes. Lymph nodes in the ileum are associated with those of the large intestine.

A blind caecum is attached to the mesentery in the 20-metre-long large intestine of the dromedary. A large-diameter colon is situated on the left side of the abdomen in a large mesenteric fold. Most of the water absorption by the camel intestine is at the point where the colon narrows. The lymph supply of the large intestine is mainly at two sites, these being at the entrance and close to the terminal portion where the colon passes into the rectum.

5.2.5   Liver, Pancreas and Spleen

The liver is very much lobulated with a great deal of interlobular tissue. The bile and pancreatic ducts are common as they enter the duodenum. The spleen is not attached to the diaphragm but is high on the left side of the rumen. The peritoneum is similar to that of cattle but there is no gall bladder.

5.3   Nutritional Physiology of Camelids

Differences occur in nitrogen, glucose, fatty acid and ketone metabolism between the Camelidae and the true ruminants. The forestomach proportions of volatile fatty acids (VFA) are, however, similar, this having been interpreted as an indication that metabolic processes are similar in the two groups (Maloiy 1972b).

5.3.1   Motility

Motility in the camel stomach differs from that of ruminants. In compartments 1 and 2 the cyclical pattern of motility has been categorized into A and B contractions. Each cycle starts with a strong contraction in the canal between compartments 2 and 3. This is followed by a single rapid contraction in C2, then there is a short relaxed phase of the canal prior to a further contraction, during which stage C2 relaxes while the caudal portion of C1 contracts. The proximal part of the canal thus contracts before the distal part. A typical motility cycle is comprised of seven A-type and five B-type contractions (Fig. 5.3) and lasts for about 3 to 4minutes in camels, including the resting phase. In llama each cycle lasts only about 1.5minutes (Vallenas and Stevens 1971; Heller, Lechner and von Engelhardt 1986). Filling of C2 with food decreases the number of contractions per cycle but increases the rate of cycling. The strong contractions push food round C1 in an anticlockwise direction, squeezing out fluid, which is absorbed in the glandular sac region.

Contractions along the length of C3 occur continuously. Although it was originally thought that movement was not peristaltic (Ehrlein and von Engelhardt 1971), at least in the llama, it appears that in the camel the movements are peristaltic (Heller, Lechner and von Engelhardt 1986).

5.3.2   Movement of Digesta

The contents of the forestomach (C1 and C2) pass to the hind stomach (C3) when the strong contraction of C2 causes an expansion of the connecting canal. Canal motility is therefore responsible for the flow of digesta from the forestomach to the lower part of the gastro-intestinal tract. In llama, the flow rate is estimated at 850ml/h equivalent to about 17ml at each contraction (von Engelhardt, Ali and Wipper 1979).

Particle size varies from 0.1mm to 10.0mm in the forestomach (C1 and C2). The maximum size of particles which can pass from the forestomach to the lower parts of the alimentary tract is from 3mm to 5mm in camels. The particle size tends to increase with an increased fibre content of the diet.

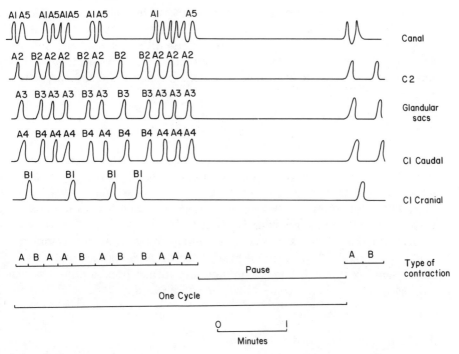

Fig. 5.3. Forestomach motility patterns in the camel (Heller, Lechner and von Engelhardt 1986)

5.3.3 Retention Time

A limiting factor to the utilization of cellulose from cell wall constituents is the slow rate of microbial breakdown. Retention time of feed particles in the fermentation chamber of the forestomach is therefore important as it largely governs the amount of fibre digested. A longer retention time is a prerequisite for efficient digestion of fibrous diets. In the forestomach of the dromedary, small particles are retained for 41 hours while larger particles are retained on average for 57 hours (Heller et al. 1986). This is longer than in other camelids where, for example, small particles are retained for 29 hours in the llama and water for 15 hours. Camels have longer retention times than conventional domestic ruminants and can therefore be expected to be more efficient in digestion of fibre. Fluid is retained in the forestomach of the dromedary for only 14 hours, this being shorter than that of the llama and of other domestic ruminants. High fluid turnover rates support a more rapid microbial fermentation through a higher buffering capacity and improve outflow of the soluble products of microbial metabolism.

Two major factors appear to be implicated in the selective retention of large particles in C1 and C2 so that they can undergo further breakdown. These factors are an unequal distribution of the particles and canal motility. Large particles that do succeed in passing into C3 may be held as much as ten times longer than small particles and fluid in the omasum/abomasum area.

5.3.4   Rumination

Regurgitation of the food bolus occurs at maximum contraction of the upper part of the rumen. The contents are moved towards the cardiac area at this stage. Eructation of the gaseous products of digestion and fermentation takes place at the same time as the contraction of the caudal part of the reticulo-rumen, while the cranial portion is relaxed.

Reduction in particle size is achieved initially by chewing, and rumination is therefore essential for efficient breakdown of particle size. Total chewing time might eventually become a limitation to further breakdown of particle size. Most rumination in camels that are herded by day takes place at night.

5.3.5   Rumen Chemistry

There is a high concentration of short-chain fatty acids in the camel rumen. Fermentation rates and pH are similar to those observed for cattle. It appears that the differences in stomach morphology between camelids and ruminants do not influence the fermentation rate but, as noted, fluid and small particle outflow is faster.

Ruminal protozoa differ in camels from those observed in sheep (Abou Akkada 1986). *Entodinium* sp. account for about 75 of all protozoa in both camels and sheep when fully hydrated, but this species drops to 68% in water-deprived sheep while it increases to 84% in dehydrated camels. *Entodinium* is largely responsible for the digestion of the starch fraction of the diet. *Epidinium. Metadinium* and *Eudiplodinium* account for the rest of the ciliate protozoa in camels, while *Diplodinium* forms the bulk of the non-*Entodinium* population in sheep. The high levels of *Entodinium* and *Epidinium* in the forestomach of the camel indicate an ability to digest efficiently the complex polysaccharides, the nitrogen materials and the lipid containing chloroplasts of the ingested plant material.

Absorption rates of VFA, sodium and chloride are two to three times faster in the forestomach of the camel than they are in goats and sheep (Maloiy and Clemens 1980). Farther back in the alimentary canal, other solutes and water are rapidly absorbed. About 60% of the sodium, 70% of VFA and 30% of water are absorbed in the forestomach. Acidification is high in the hind stomach with high concentrations of chlorine.

Camels are well adapted to low protein diets but this is assisted to some extent by their ability to select high-quality material. The recycling rate of urea increases under stress, this first being demonstrated in a pregnant camel which excreted very little urea in its urine (Schmidt-Nielsen 1959). Recycling efficiency of urea increases from 47 to 86% in camels in which dietary protein is reduced from 13.6 to 6.1 %. In llama fed a diet with high energy but low protein the urea recycling rate can reach 95%. In llama fed diets containing the same level of energy but different levels of protein, animals on a low protein diet used 78% of nitrogen from recycled urea in metabolism, but animals fed a diet adequate in protein used only 10% of recycled urea nitrogen.

The blood concentration of urea does not apparently affect the amount of urea returned to the alimentary canal. It seems that the permeability of the stomach lining to urea changes with the type of diet fed. Most recycled urea is absorbed in the forestomach where both VFA and CO_2 levels influence permeability. High concentrations of VFA increase the rate of absorption, with butyric acid having a greater effect than either acetic or propionic acid.

The Camelidae appear to be significantly more efficient in digesting dry matter, fibre, cellulose and crude protein than other ruminants and domestic non-ruminants (Hintz, Schryver and Halberd 1973). This is probably due to the rapid and frequent cycling of the stomach contents.

5.4 Domestic Small Ruminants

In East African hair sheep and goats, in spite of their different dietary preferences and feeding habits, the contents of the reticulo-rumen do not differ between the species as a percentage of fresh body weight (Hoppe, Qvortrup and Woodford 1977). In both species, fermentation rates of the rumen contents were slower than those found in wild ruminants feeding in the same area and with access to the same resources. The slow fermentation rates were attributed to both these species being less selective of easily fermentable plants and plant parts and more adapted to coarse roughage because of their significantly higher rumen content:live weight ratio when compared with the wild ruminants. The pH of the rumen fluid was, however, similar in all species (5.6–6.5) and there were no differences in ammonia nitrogen content. Sheep differed from impala in total VFA content of the rumen, but in all species the molar proportion of the different fatty acids did not differ. Acetic acid was 77% of total VFA in both goats and sheep, with propionic and butyric acids being next most important. The high proportion of acetic acid probably results from the high fibre level in the diet.

Although the fermentation rate in goats and sheep was slow, total gas production was similar to that in the wild ruminants because of the large rumen size. It is evident, therefore, that a large rumen coupled with a slow fermentation rate is one adaptive strategy for ruminants in dry areas.

Desert small ruminants are better adapted to poor quality diets than non-adapted ones, and also eat less in relation to body weight. Lower feed consumption in desert-adapted goats is due to a lower basal metabolic rate (Shkolnik, Borut and Choshniak 1972). Digestibility of feed is higher in adapted than in non-adapted goats and the former are more efficient at nitrogen conservation. On good-quality diets the differences are not marked, but on low-quality diets nitrogen intake and entry rates and cycled urea are all higher in the desert Bedouin goat than in temperate Saanen goats (Silanikove, Tagari and Shkolnik 1980). In Bedouin goats 87% of nitrogen entry was recycled compared to only 70% in Saanen, the high rate of the Bedouin goat being equalled only by the camel amongst other ruminants. The recycled nitrogen assists in improving the digestibility of the poor quality diet and thus helps the goat to meet its energy demands as well. The two characteristics of economic nitrogen metabolism and efficient recycling acting on roughage to provide an increased energy supply complement each other in the adaptive features of the Bedouin goat to the desert environment.

5.5 Wild Ruminants

Most wild ruminants in dry areas have adopted a strategy of a fast fermentation rate and a low rumen content to body weight ratio. It is possible that the low weight of the rumen content allows greater mobility of the animal to search for food. Compared to the approximately 18% of body weight of the reticulo-rumen contents of goats and sheep, that of Thomson's gazelle is only 12% and that of Grant's gazelle and of impala is 9% and 7% respectively (Hoppe, Qvortrup and Woodford 1977). All these three species have rapid fermentation rates which are significantly faster than in goats and sheep. The rapid fermentation rate requires a rapid removal rate in order to maintain pH in the region of 5.5 to 6.4.

Total VFA concentrations for a number of species range from 67mEq/litre to 199mEq/litre (Hoppe 1984). Levels are lower in an individual species in the dry period than they are in the wet period. There are no constant differences between the three major types (roughage, intermediate and concentrate selectors) of feeders. In extreme concentrate selectors like the dik-dik, however, dry season fermentation rates are more than three times higher than in the buffalo (Maloiy, Clemens and Kamau 1982; Hoppe et al. 1983). A fast rate of VFA absorption is aided by a mass of rumen papillae which are found on the dorsal rumen wall in concentrate selectors as opposed to a smooth surface in the slow-fermenting domestic ruminant. In order to be able to maintain high fermentation rates to provide energy to support a high basal metabolic rate, dik-dik not only select a rapidly fermentable substrate but eat and ruminate often throughout the day and night. The retention time in dik-dik is very short and, because of the highly selected diet, cellulose is of little importance in this species. Unlike most other ruminants, therefore, dik-dik have either no rumen protozoa or have only *Entodinium*.

Acetate is the fatty acid which contributes most to molar percentage in all three types of feeder. Of a range of species, acetic acid was lowest in gerenuk (*Litocranius walleri*) at 65% molar proportion. Butyric acid levels are highest, in general, in roughage feeders because of the concentrations of butyrate-producing protozoa in the rumen. High butyric levels are also found in some concentrate selectors such as kudu (*Tragelaphus* spp.) and giraffe (*Giraffa camelopardalis*).

Mean retention times of particles in the rumen are longest in roughage feeders, intermediate in intermediate feeders and shortest in concentrate selectors. In Kalahari gemsbok, for example, the mean retention time is 75 hours, in giraffe it is 69 hours, in eland 57 hours and, as we have seen, is very much shorter (about 12–20 hours) in dik-dik. Prolonged retention times are often a response to high fibre diets even in the more dietarily efficient concentrate selectors. A longer retention time will, however, eventually decrease intake and cause starvation. This is probably a principal reason why desert ruminants are either concentrate selectors or intermediate feeders rather than roughage feeders.

References

Abdel-Gadir SE, Wahabi A, Idris OM (1984) A note on the haematology of adult Sudanese dromedaries. In: Cockrill WR (ed) The Camelid, an all-purpose animal. Scand Inst Afr Stud, Uppsala, pp 444–448

Abou Akkada AR (1986) The nutrition of Arabian camel (dromedary). Fac Agric, Alexandria University, Alexandria (mimeo)

Adolph EF (1981) Regulation of intake. Clearances. Am J Physiol 240:356–363R

Adolph EF (1982) Termination of drinking. Satiation. Fed Proc 41:2533–2535

Bagnouls F, Gaussen H (1953) Saison sèche et indice xerothermique. Bull Soc Hist Nat Toulouse 88:193–239

Bagnouls F, Gaussen H (1957) Les climats biologiques et leur classification. Ann Geogr 66:193–220

Baker MA (1979) A brain cooling system in mammals. Sci Am 24:114–122

Baker MA, Hayward JN (1968) The influence of the nasal mucosa and the carotid rete upon hypothalamic temperature in sheep. J Physiol Lond 198:561–579

Banerjee S, Bhattacharjee RC, Singh TI (1962) Hematological studies in the normal adult Indian camel (Camelus dromedarius). Am J Physiol 203:1185–1187

Bartels H, Hilpert P, Barbey K, Beke K, Reigel K, Lang EM, Metcalfe J (1963) Respiratory functions of blood of the yak, llama, camel, Dzbowski deer and African elephant. Am J Physiol 205:331–336

Bartholomew GA, White FN, Howell TR (1976) The thermal significance of the nest of the sociable weaver Philetairus socius: summer observations. Ibis 118:402–410

Bianca W (1970) Effects of dehydration, rehydration and overhydration on the blood and urine of oxen. Br Vet J 126:121–132

Blair-West JR, Brook AH, Simpson PA (1972) Renin responses to water restriction and rehydration. J Physiol 226:1–13

Blair-West JR, Brook AH, Gibson A, Morris M, Pullan JP (1979) Renin, antidiuretic hormone and kidney in water restriction and water dehydration. J Physiol 294:181–193

Bligh J (1972) Evaporative heat loss in hot arid environments. Symp Zool Soc Lond 31:357–369

Borut A, Dmi'el R, Shkolnik A (1979) Heat balance of resting and walking goats: comparison of climatic chamber and exposure in the desert. Physiol Zool 52:105–112

Bradshaw SD (1986) Ecophysiology of desert reptiles. Academic Press, London

Brockway JM, McDonald JD, Pullar JD (1963) The energy cost of reproduction in sheep. J Physiol Lond 167:318–327

Brown GD (1974) Heat tolerance and animal productivity in the Australian arid zone. In: Wilson AD (ed) Studies of the Australian arid zone. II. Animal production. Common Sci and Indust Res Organ, Canberra, pp 23–36

Buxton PA (1923) Animal life in deserts, a study of the fauna in relation to the environment. Arnold, London

Cena K, Monteith JL (1975) Transfer processes in animal coats. I. Radiative transfer. Proc R Soc Lond 188B:377–394

Charnot Y (1958) Repeicussions de la deshydration sur la biochimie et l'endocrinologie du dromadaire. Thèse, Université de Paris VI, Paris

Charnot Y (1961) Equilibre minéral tissulaire dans la deshydration du dromadaire. J Physiol Paris 58:793–806

Charnot Y (1967) Regulation endocrinienne du métabolisme de l'eau chez le dromadaire. Bull Soc Sci Nat Phys Maroc 47:1–7

Chavanne P, Boue A (1950) Taux normaux de l'urée et du glucose sanguin chez le dromadaire nord-africain. Rev Elev Med Vet Pays Trop 4:183

Choshniak I, Shkolnik A (1977) Rapid rehydration in the black Bedouin goat: red blood cells fragility and the role of the rumen. Comp Biochem Physiol 56A:581–583

Choshniak I, Shkolnik A (1978) The rumen as a protective osmotic mechanism during rapid rehydration in the black Bedouin goat. In: Skadhange E, Jorgensen CB (eds) Osmotic and volume regulation (Alfred Benzon Symposium Volume II). Munksgaard, Copenhagen, pp 344–346

Choshniak I, Wittenberg C, Rosenfeld J, Shkolnik A (1984) Rapid rehydration and kidney function in the black Bedouin goat. Physiol Zool 57:573–579

Choshniak I, Wittenberg C, Saham D (1987) Rehydrating Bedouin goats with saline: rumen and kidney function. Physiol Zool 60:373–378

Cloudsley-Thompson JL (1965) The fauna of Jebel Marra, Western Sudan. Sudan Silva 2(16):24–28

Cloudsley-Thompson JL (1977) Man and the biology of arid zones. Arnold, London

Cole DP (1975) Nomads of the nomads. The Al-Murrah Bedouin of the Empty Quarter. Adline, Chicago

Coppock DL, Ellis JE, Swift DM (1988) Seasonal patterns of activity, travel and water intake for livestock in South Turkana, Kenya. J Arid Environ 14:319–331

Dahlborn IL, Robertshaw D, Schroter RC, Filali RZ (1987) Effects of dehydration and heat stress on brain and body temperature in the camel. J Physiol Lond 388:28P

Daniel PM, Dawes DK, Pritchard MML (1953) Studies of the carotid rete and its associated arteries. Phil Trans R Soc 237B:173–215

Davies R (1957) The camel's back. Murray, London

Degen AA (1977a) Fat-tailed Awassi and German mutton Merino sheep under semi-arid conditions. 1. Total body water, its distribution and turnover. J Agric Sci Camb 88:693–698

Degen AA (1977b) Fat-tailed Awassi and German mutton Merino sheep under semi-arid conditions. 2. Total body water and water turnover during pregnancy and lactation. J Agric Sci Camb 88:699–704

Degen AA (1977c) Fat-tailed Awassi and German mutton Marino sheep under semi-arid conditions. 3. Body temperature and panting rate. J Agric Sci Camb 89:399–405

Dixon JEW, Louw GN (1978) Seasonal effects on nutrition, reproduction and aspects of thermoregulation in the Namaqua sandgrouse (*Pterocles namaqua*). Madoqua 11:19–29

Dmi'el R, Robertshaw D, Choshniak I (1980) Is a black coat in the desert a means of saving metabolic energy? Nature (Lond) 283:761–762

Dowling DK, Nay Y (1962) Hair follicles and sweat glands of the camel (*Camelus dromedarius*). Nature (Lond) 195:578–580

Edney EB (1971) The body temperature of Tenebrionid beetles in the Namib Desert of southern Africa. J Exp Biol 55: 253–272

Ehrlein HJ, Engelhardt W von (1971) Studies on the gastric motility of the llama. Zentralbl Vet Med 18A:181–191

Elder WH, Rodgers DH (1975) Body temperature in the African elephant as related to ambient temperature. Mammalia 39:395–399

Engelhardt W von, Heller R (1985) Structure and function of the forestomach in camelids – a comparative approach. Acta Physiol Scand 124 Suppl: 542

Engelhardt W von, Sallman D (1972) Resorption und Sekretion im Pansen des Guanacos (*Lama guanocoe*). Zentralbl Vet Med 19A:117–131

Engelhardt W von, Ali KE, Wipper E (1979) Absorption and secretion in the tubiform forestomach (compartment 3) of the llama. J Comp Physiol 132B:337–341

Etzion Z, Yagil R (1986) Renal function in camels (*Camelus dromedarius*) following rapid rehydration. Physiol Zool 59:558–562

Etzion Z, Meyerstein N, Yagil R (1984) Tritiated water metabolism during dehydration and rehydration in the camel. J Appl Physiol 56:217–220

Finberg JPM, Yagil R, Berlyne GM (1978) Response of the renin-aldosterone system in the camel to acute dehydration. J Appl Physiol (Respir Environ Excercise Physiol) 44:926–930

Finch VA (1972a) Thermoregulation and heat balance of the East African eland and hartebeest. Am J Physiol 222:1374–1377

Finch VA (1972b) Energy exchanges with the environment of two East African antelopes, the eland and the hartebeest. Symp Zool Soc Lond 31:315–326

Finch VA (1976) An assessment of the energy budget of Boran cattle. J Thermal Biol 1:143–148

Finch VA, King JM (1982) Energy-conserving mechanisms as adaptation to undernutrition and water deprivation in the African zebu. In: Use of tritiated water in studies of production and adaptation in ruminants. Int Atomic Energy Agency, Vienna, pp 167–178

Finch VA, Western D (1977) Cattle colours in pastoral herds: natural selection or social preference? Ecology 58:1384–1392

Finch VA, Dmi'el R, Boxman R, Shkolnik A, Taylor CR (1980) Why black goats in hot deserts? Effects of coat colour on heat exchanges of wild and domestic goats. Physiol Zool 53:19–25

Finch VA, Bennett IL, Holmes CR (1982) Sweating response in cattle and its relation to rectal temperature, tolerance of sun and metabolic rate. J Agric Sci Camb 99:479–487

Folk GE Jr (1966) Introduction to environmental physiology. Lea and Febiger, Philadelphia

French MH (1956) The effects of infrequent water intake on the consumption and digestibility of hay by Zebu cattle. Emp J Exp Agric 24:128–136

Fuglestad F (1974) La famine de 1931 dans l'ouest nigérien: reflexions autour d'une catastrophe naturelle. Rev Fr Hist Outre-Mer 61(222):18–33

Gatenby RM (1979) Water in the heat budget of ruminant skin and coat. Thesis, University of Nottingham, Nottingham

Gatenby RM (1986) Exponential relation between sweat rate and skin temperature in hot climates. J Agric Sci Camb 106:175–183

Gauthier-Pilters H (1958) Quelques observations sur l'écologie et l'ethologie du dromadaire dans le Sahara nord-occidental. Mammalia 22:294–316

Gauthier-Pilters H (1969) Observations sur l'écologie du dromadaire en Moyenne Mauritanie. Bull IFAN 31A:1259-1380

Ghobrial LI (1970a) The water relations of the desert antelope, *Gazella dorcas dorcas*. Physiol Zool 43:249–256

Ghobrial LI (1970b) A comparative study of the integument of the camel, Dorcas gazelle and jerboa in relation to desert life. J Zool Lond 160:509–521

Ghobrial LI (1974) Water relations and requirements of the Dorcas gazelle in Sudan. Mammalia 38:88–107

Ghodsian J, Nowrouzi I, Schels HF (1978) Study of some haematological parameters in Iranian camel. Trop Anim Hlth Prod 10:109–110

Ghosh PK, Khan MS, Abichandani RK (1976) Effect of short-term water deprivation in summer on Marwari sheep. J Agric Sci Camb 87:221–223

Goodall AM (1955) Arterio-venous anastomoses in the skin of the head and ears of the calf. J Anat 89:100

Goodall DW, Perry RA, Howes KMW (eds) (1979) Arid land ecosystems: structure functioning and management. Cambridge University Press, Cambridge

Goyal SP, Ghosh PK (1987) A note on the measurement of heat exchange by radiotelemetry in black desert goats during winter. J Agric Sci Camb 108:509–510

Grettenberger J (1987) Ecology of the Dorcas gazelle in northern Niger. Mammalia 51:527–536

Hadley NF (1972) Desert species and adaptation. Am Sci 60:338–347

Hadley NF (ed) (1975) Environmental physiology of desert organisms. Dowden, Hutchinson and Ross, Stroudsberg

Hales JRS, Webster MED (1967) Respiratory function during thermal tachypnoea in sheep. J Physiol London 190:241–260

Hamilton WJ, Seely MK (1976) Fog basking by the Namib desert beetle, *Onymacris unguicularis*. Nature (Lond) 262:284–285

Heath JE (1964) Head-body differences in horned lizards. Physiol Zool 37:273–279

Heath JE (1966) Venous shunts in the cephalic sinuses of horned lizards. Physiol Zool 39:30–35

Heckler JF, Budtz-Olsen OE, Ostwald M (1964) The rumen as a water store in sheep. Aust J Agric Res 15:961–968

Heller R, Lechner M, Engelhardt W von (1986) Forestomach motility in the camel (*Camelus dromedarius*). Comp Biochem Physiol 84A:285–288

Heller R, Lechner M, Weyreter H, Engelhardt W von (1986) Forestomach fluid volume and retention of fluid and particles in the gastrointestinal tract of the camel (*Camelus dromedarius*). Zentralbl Vet Med 33A:396–399

Hiley PG (1975) How the elephant keeps its cool. Nat Hist New York 84(10):34–41

Hintz HF, Schryver HF, Halbert M (1973) A note on the comparison of digestion by New World camels, sheep and ponies. Anim Prod 16:303–305

Hofmann RR (1973) The ruminant stomach. East Afr Lit Bur, Nairobi

Hofmann RR, Stewart DRM (1972) Grazers or browsers: a classification based on the stomach-structure and feeding habit of East African ruminants. Mammalia 36:226–240

Hofmeyr MD, Louw GN (1987) Thermoregulation, pelage conductance and renal function in the desert-adapted springbok, *Antidorcas marsupialis*. J Arid Environ 13:137–151

Hollerman DF, Dieterich RA (1973) Body water content and turnover in several species of rodents as evaluated by the tritiated water method. J Mammal 54:456–465

Hoppe PP (1976) Tritiated water turnover in Kirk's dik-dik, *Madoqua (Rhyncotragus) kirkii*, Gunther, 1880. Säugetierkd Mitt 24:318–319

Hoppe PP (1977) How to survive heat and aridity: ecophysiology of the dik-dik antelope. Vet Med Rev 8:77–86

Hoppe PP (1984) Strategies of digestion in Africa herbivores. In: Gilchrist FM, Mackie RI (eds) Herbivore nutrition in the subtropics and tropics. Science Press (Pty), Craighall (South Africa), pp 222–243

Hoppe PP, Kay NB, Maloiy GMO (1974) Salivary secretion in the camel. J Physiol 224:32–33

Hoppe PP, Johansen K, Musewe V, Maloiy GMO (1975) Thermal panting reduces oxygen uptake in the dik-dik. Acta Physiol Scand 95(2):9A

Hoppe PP, Kay NB, Maloiy GMO (1975) The rumen as a reservoir during dehydration and rehydration in the camel. J Physiol 254:76–77

Hoppe PP, Qvortrup SA, Woodford MH (1977) Rumen fermentation and food selection in East African sheep, goats, Thomson's gazelle, Grant's gazelle and impala. J Agric Sci Camb 89:129–135

Hoppe PP, Hoven W van, Engelhardt W von, Prins R, Lankhorst A (1983) Pregastric and caecal fermentation in dik-dik (*Rhyncotragus kirkii*) and suni (*Nesotragus moschatus*). Comp Biochem Physiol 75A:517–524

Horowitz M, Adler JH (1983) Plasma volume regulation during heat stress: albumin synthesis vs. capillary permeability. A comparison between desert and non-desert species. Comp Biochem Physiol 75A:105–110

Horrocks D, Phillips GD (1961) Factors affecting the water and food intakes of European and zebu-type cattle. J Agric Sci Camb 56:379–381

Hutchinson JCD, Allen TE, Spence FB (1975) Measurement of the reflectances for solar radiation of the coats of live animals. Comp Biochem Physiol 50A:343–349

Jackson DC, Schmidt-Nielsen K (1964) Countercurrent heat exchange in the respiratory passages. Proc Nat Acad Sci 51:1192–1197

Jarman PJ (1973) The free water intake of impala in relation to the water content of their food. E Afr Agric For J 38:343–351

Jenkinson DMc (1969) Sweat gland function in domestic animals. In: Botelho SY, Brooks FP, Shelley WB (eds) The exocrine glands. University of Pennsylvania Press, Philadelphia, pp 201–221

Jenkinson DMc (1972) Evaporative temperature regulation in domestic animals. Symp Zool Soc Lond 31:345–356

Jenkinson DMc, Robertshaw D (1971) Studies on the nature of sweat gland "fatigue" in the goat. J Physiol Lond 212:455–465

Kennedy PM, Macfarlane WV (1971) Oxygen consumption and water turnover of the fat-tailed marsupials *Dasycercus cristicauda* and *Sminthopsis crassicaudata*. Comp Biochem Physiol 40A:723–732

Khan MS, Ghosh PK (1982) Comparative physiology of water economy in desert sheep and goats. Proc III Int Conf Goat Prod Dis, 10–15 Jan 1982, Tucson, Arizona, p 337

Khan MS, Ghosh PK, Sasidharan TO (1978) Effect of acute water restriction on plasma proteins and on blood and urinary electrolytes in Barmer goats of the Rajasthan desert. J Agric Sci Camb 91:395–398

Khan MS, Sasidharan TO, Ghosh PK (1979) Glomerular filtration rate and blood and urinary urea concentrations in Barmer goats of the Rajasthan desert. J Agric Sci Camb 93:247–248

King JM (1979) Game domestication for animal production in Kenya: field studies of the body-water turnover of game and livestock. J Agric Sci Camb 93:71–79

King JM (1983) Livestock water needs in pastoral Africa in relation to climate and forage (Research Report No 7). Int Livestock Cent Afr, Addis Ababa

King JM, Kingaby GP, Colvin JG, Heath BR (1975) Seasonal variation in water turnover by oryx and eland on the Galana Game Ranch Research Project. E Afr Wild J 13:287–296

Kleiber M (1961) The fire of life. An introduction to animal energetics. Wiley, New York

Kohli RN (1963) Cellular micrometry of camel's blood. Ind Vet J 40:134–137

Kumar M, Banerjee S (1962) Biochemical studies on the Indian camel (*Camelus dromedarius*) 3. Plasma-insulin like activity and glucose tolerance. J Sci Indust Res 21C:291–292

Lamprey HF (1963) Ecological separation of the large mammal species in the Tarangire Game Reserve, Tanganyika. E Afr Wild J 1:63–92

Lamprey HF (1964) Estimation of the large mammal densities, biomass and energy exchange in the Tarangire Game Reserve and the Masai steppe in Tanganyika. E Afr Wild J 2:1–46

Langer P (1984) Anatomical and nutritional adaptations of wild herbivores. In: Gilchrist FM, Mackie RI (eds) Herbivore nutrition in the subtropics and tropics. Science Press (Pty), Craighall (South Africa), pp 185–203

Lee DG, Schmidt-Nielsen K (1962) The skin, sweat glands and hair follicles of the camel (*Camelus dromedarius*). Anat Rec 143:71–77

Leese AS (1927) A treatise on the one-humped camel in health and disease. Haynes and Son, Stamford, UK

Le Houérou HN (1979) North Africa. In: Goodall DW, Perry, RA, Howes KMW (eds) Arid land ecosystems: structure, functioning and management. Cambridge University Press, Cambridge

Leitch I, Thompson JS (1945) The water economy of farm animals. Nutr Abst Rev 14:197–223

Leonard AG (1894) The camel. Its uses and management. Longmans, London

Lewis JG (1977) Game domestication for animal production in Kenya: activity patterns of eland, oryx, buffalo and zebu cattle. J Agric Sci Camb 89:551–563

Lewis JG (1978) Game domestication for animal production in Kenya: shade behaviour and factors affecting the herding of eland, oryx, buffalo and zebu cattle. J Agric Sci Camb 90:587–595

Lewis JG, Wilson RT (1979) The ecology of Swayne's hartebeest. Biol Conserv 15:1–12

Livingston HC, Payne WJA, Friend MT (1964) Nitrogen metabolism of cattle in East Africa. The problem and the experimental procedure. J Agric Sci Camb 62:313–319

Louw GN, Belonje PC, Coetzee HJ (1969) Renal function, respiration, heart rate and thermoregulation in the ostrich (*Struthio camelus*). Sci Pap Namib Desert Res Station 42:43–54

Louw GN, Seely MK (1982) Ecology of desert organisms. Longmans, London

MAB (1979) Map of the world distribution of arid regions (MAB Technical Notes No 7). U N Educ, Soc Cult Organ, Paris

Macfarlane WV (1964) Terrestrial animals in dry heat: ungulates (Handbook of physiology, adaptation to the environment). Am Physiol Soc, Washington DC

Macfarlane WV (1968) Comparative functions of ruminants in hot environments. In: Hafez ESE (ed) Adaptation of domestic animals. Lea and Febiger, Philadelphia, pp 264–276

Macfarlane WV (1977) Survival in an arid land. The desert mouse and the camel. Aust Nat Hist 29:18–23

Macfarlane WV, Howard B (1966) Water content and turnover of identical twin *Bos indicus* and *B. taurus* in Kenya. J Agric Sci Camb 66:297–302

Macfarlane WV, Howard B (1972) Comparative water and energy economy of wild and domestic animals. Symp Zool Soc Lond 31:261–296

Macfarlane WV, Howard B (1974) Ruminant water metabolism in arid areas. In: Wilson AD (ed) Studies of the Australian arid zone. II. Animal production. Commonw Sci Indust Res Organ, Canberra, pp 7–22

Macfarlane WV, Morris RJH, Howard B (1962) Water metabolism of Merino sheep and camels. Austr J Sci 25:112–116

Macfarlane WV, Morris RJH, Howard B (1963) Turnover and distribution of water in desert camels, sheep, cattle and kangaroos. Nature (Lond) 197:270–271

Macfarlane WV, Howard B, Morris RJH (1966) Water metabolism of Merino sheep shorn in summer. Aust J Agric Res 18:947–958

Macfarlane WV, Howard B, Siebert BD (1969) Tritiated water used to measure intake of milk and tissue growth of ruminants in the field. Nature (Lond) 221:578

Macfarlane WV, Howard B, Haines H, Kennedy PJ, Sharpe CM (1971) Hierarchy of water and energy turnover of desert mammals. Nature (Lond) 234:483–484

McDowell RE (1972) Improvement of livestock production in warm climates. Freeman, San Francisco

McGinnies WG (1979) Description and structure of arid ecosystems: general description of desert areas. In: Goodall DW, Perry RA, Howes KMW (eds) Arid-land ecosystems: structure, functioning and management. Cambridge University Press, Cambridge

Maloiy GMO (1970) Water economy of the Somali donkey. Am J Physiol 219:1522–1527

Maloiy GMO (ed) (1972a) Comparative physiology of desert animals (Symp Zool Soc Lond, No 31). Academic Press, London

Maloiy GMO (1972b) Comparative studies on digestion and fermentation rate in the fore-stomach of the one-humped camel and the zebu steer. Res Vet Sci 13:476–481

Maloiy GMO (1972c) Renal salt and water excretion in the camel (*Camelus dromedarius*). Symp Zool Soc Lond 31:243–259

Maloiy GMO (1973a) The water metabolism of a small East African antelope: the dik-dik. Proc R Soc Lond 184B:167–178

Maloiy GMO (1973b) Water metabolism of East African ruminants in arid and semi-arid regions. Z Tierz Züchtungsbiol 90:219–228

Maloiy GMO, Clemens ET (1980) Colonic absorption and secretion of electrolytes as seen in five species of East African herbivorous mammals. Comp Biochem Physiol 67A:21–25

Maloiy GMO, Hopcraft D (1971) Thermoregulation and water relations of two East African antelopes: the hartebeest and impala. Comp Biochem Physiol 38A:525–534

Maloiy GMO, Taylor CR (1971) Water requirements of African goats and haired-sheep. J Agric Sci Camb 77:203–208

Maloiy GMO, Taylor CR, Clemens ET (1978) A comparison of gastrointestinal water content and osmolality in East African herbivores during hydration and dehydration. J Agric Sci Camb 91:249–254

Maloiy GMO, Macfarlane WV, Shkolnik A (1979) Mammalian herbivores. In: Maloiy GMO (ed) Comparative physiology of osmoregulation in animals, Volume II. Academic Press, London, pp 185–209

Maloiy GMO, Clemens ET, Kamau JMZ (1982) Aspects of digestion and in vitro rumen fermentation rate in six species of East African wild ruminants. J Zool Lond 197:345–353

Maltz E, Shkolnik A (1980) Milk production in the desert: lactation and water economy in the black Bedouin goat. Physiol Zool 53:12–18

Maltz E, Olsson K, Glick SM, Fyhrquist F, Silanikove N, Choshniak L, Shkolnik A (1984) Homeostatic responses to water deprivation or hemorrhage in lactating and non-lactating Bedouin goats. Comp Biochem Physiol 77A:79–84

Marder J (1973) Body temperature regulation in the brown-necked raven (*Corvus corax ruficollis*). II. Thermal changes in the plumage of ravens exposed to solar radiation. Comp Biochem Physiol 45A:431–440

Mares RG (1954) Animal husbandry, animal industry and animal disease in the Somaliland Protectorate. Br Vet J 110:422–423; 470–480

Meigs P (1952) World distribution of arid and semi-arid homoclimates. Arid Zone Res 1:203–210

Monod T (1955) Longs trajets chameliers. Bull Liais Sahara 20:39–42

Monod T (1973) Les déserts. Horizons de France, Paris

More T, Sahni KL (1980) Effect of water deprivation on blood and urine components of lactating sheep under semi-desert conditions. Ind J Anim Sci 50:411–416

Nawar SMA, El-Khaligi GEM (1975) Morphological, micromorphological and histochemical studies on the parotid salivary glands of the one-humped camel (*Camelus dromedarius*). Gegenbaurs Morphol Jahrb 121:430–439

Nicholson MJ (1987) The effect of drinking frequency on some aspects of the productivity of zebu cattle. J Agric Sci Camb 108:119–128

Noy-Meir I (1973) Desert ecosystems: environment and producers. Ann Rev Ecol Syst 4:25–51

Oliver J (1965) Guide to the natural history of Khartoum Province. II. The climate of Khartoum province. Sudan Notes Rec 46:1–40

Payne WJA (1964) The origin of domestic cattle in Africa. Emp J Exp Agric 32:97–112

Payne WJA, Hutchinson HG (1963) Water metabolism of cattle in East Africa. The problem and the experimental procedure. J Agric Sci Camb 61:255–266

Peacock CP (1984) Sheep and goat production on Masai group ranches. Thesis, University of Reading, Reading

Peck EF (1939) Salt intake in relation to cutaneous necrosis and arthritis of one-humped camels (*Camelus dromedarius*) in British Somaliland. Vet Rec 51:1355–1360

Perk K (1963) The camel's erythrocyte. Nature (Lond) 200:272–273

Perk K (1966) Osmotic hemolysis of the camel's erythrocytes. 1. A micro-cinematographic study. J Exp Zool 163:241–246

Perk K, Frei YF, Herz A (1964) Osmotic fragility of red blood cells of young and mature domestic and laboratory animals. Am J Vet Res 25:1241–1248

Phillips GD (1960) The relationship between water and food intakes of European and Zebu type steers. J Agric Sci Camb 54:231–234

Quartermain AR (1964) Heat tolerance in Southern Rhodesian sheep fed on a maintenance diet. J Agric Sci Camb 62:333–339

Quezel P (1965) La vegetation du Sahara du Tchad à la Mauritanie. Fischer, Stuttgart

Riquier J, Rossetti C (1976) Considérations méthodologiques sur l'établissement d'une carte des risques de désertification (Rapp Consult Tech). Food Agric Organ, Rome (mimeo)

Robertshaw D (1968) The pattern and control of sweating in the sheep and goat. J Physiol Lond 198:531–539

Robertshaw D, Finch VA (1976) The effects of climate on the productivity of beef cattle. In: Smith AJ (ed) Beef cattle production in developing countries. Cent Trop Vet Med, Edinburgh, pp 281–293

Robertshaw D, Taylor CR (1969) A comparison of sweat gland activity in eight species of East African bovids. J Physiol Lond 203:135–143

Rollinson DHL, Injidi MH, Jenkinson DMc (1972) The distribution of nerves, monoamine oxidase and cholinesterase in the skin of the camel (*Camelus dromedarius*). Res Vet Sci 13:304–305

Roosevelt T, Heller E (1914) Life histories of African game animals. Scribner's, New York

Schmidt-Nielsen B, Schmidt-Nielsen K, Houpt TR, Jarnum SA (1956) Water balance of the camel. Am J Physiol 185:185–194

Schmidt-Nielsen K (1959) The physiology of the camel. Sci Am 200:140–151

Schmidt-Nielsen K (1964) Desert animals: physiological problems of heat and water. Clarendon, London

Schmidt-Nielsen K (1975) Animal physiology, adaptation and environment. Cambridge University Press, Cambridge

Schmidt-Nielsen K, O'Dell R (1961) Structure and concentration mechanism in the mammalian kidney. Am J Physiol 200:1119–1124

Schmidt-Nielsen K, Schmidt-Nielsen B, Houpt TR, Jarnum SA (1957a) Urea excretion in the camel. Am J Physiol 188:477–488

Schmidt-Nielsen K, Schmidt-Nielsen B, Jarnum SA, Houpt TR (1957b) Body temperature of the camel and its relation to water economy. Am J Physiol 186:103–112

Schmidt-Nielsen K, Crawford EC Jr, Newsome AE, Rawson KS, Hammel HT (1967) Metabolic rate of camels: effect of body temperature and dehydration. Am J Physiol 212:341–346

Schmidt-Nielsen K, Schroter RC, Shkolnik A (1980) Desaturaton of the exhaled air in the camel. J Physiol Lond 305:74–75

Schoen A (1968) Studies on the water balance of the East African goat. East Afr Agric For J 34:256–262

Schoen A (1969) Water conservation and the structure of the kidneys of tropical bovids. J Physiol 204:143–144

Schoen A (1972) 8tudies on the environmental physiology of a semi-desert antelope, the dik-dik. E Afr Agric For J 40:325–330

Sclater PL, Thomas O (1894-1900) The book of antelopes. Porter, London

Seckles E, Cohen R, Etzion Z, Yagil R (1979) Sweat glands in the Bedouin camel. Refu Vet 36:71

Sharma DP, Malik PD, Saprea KL (1973) Age-wise and species-wise haematological studies in farm animals. Ind J Anim Sci 43:289–295

Shkolnik A, Choshniak I (1984) Physiological responses and productivity of goats. In: Yousef MK (ed) Stress physiology of livestock (Volume 2, Ungulates). CRC Press, Boca Raton, pp 37–57

Shkolnik A, Borut A, Choshniak I (1972) Water economy of the Bedouin goat. Symp Zool Soc Lond 31:229–242

Shkolnik A, Taylor CR, Finch VA, Borut A (1980) Why do Bedouins wear black robes in hot deserts? Nature (Lond) 283:373–375

Siebert BD, Macfarlane WV (1971) Water turnover and renal function of dromedaries in the desert. Physiol Zool 44:225–240

Siebert BD, Macfarlane WV (1975) Dehydration in desert cattle and camels. Physiol Zool 48:36–48

Silanikove N, Tagari H, Shkolnik A (1980) Gross energy digestion and urea cycling in the desert black Bedouin goat. Comp Biochem Physiol 67A:215–218

Taylor CR (1966) The vascularity and possible thermoregulatory function of the horns in goats. Physiol Zool 39:127–139

Taylor CR (1968a) The minimum water requirements of some East African bovids. Symp Zool Soc Lond 21:195–206

Taylor CR (1968b) Hygroscopic food: a source of water for desert antelopes? Nature (Lond) 219:181–182

Taylor CR (1969a) The eland and the oryx. Sci Am 220:88–95

Taylor CR (1969b) Metabolism, respiratory changes and water balance of an antelope, the eland. Am J Physiol 217:317–320

Taylor CR (1970a) Strategies of temperature regulation: effect on evaporation in East African ungulates. Am J Physiol 219:1131–1135

Taylor CR (1970b) Dehydration and heat: effects on temperature regulation of East African ungulates. Am J Physiol 219:1136–1139

Taylor CR (1972) The desert gazelle: a paradox resolved. Symp Zool Soc Lond 31:215–227

Taylor CR, Lyman CP (1967) A comparative study of the environmental physiology of an East African antelope, the eland, and the Hereford steer. Physiol Zool 40:280–293

Taylor CR, Lyman CP (1972) Heat storage in running antelopes: independence of brain and body temperatures. Am J Physiol 222:114–117

Taylor CR, Spinage CA, Lyman CP (1969) Water relations of the waterbuck, an East African antelope. Am J Physiol 217:630–634

Taylor CR, Robertshaw D, Hofmann R (1969) Thermal panting: a comparison of wildebeest and zebu cattle. Am J Physiol 217:907–910

Temple RS, Thomas MER (1973) The Sahelian drought – a disaster for livestock populations. World Anim Rev 8:1–7

Thauer R (1965) Circulatory adjustments to climatic requirements (Handbook of physiology, adaptation to the environment). Am Physiol Soc, Washington DC

Thomas O, Hinton MAC (1923) On the mammals obtained in Darfur by the Lynes-Lowe expedition. Proc Zool Soc Lond 1923:247–271

Thompson GE (1976) Principles of climate physiology. In: Smith AJ (ed) Beef cattle production in developing countries. Cent Trop Vet Med, Edinburgh, pp 266–280

Thornthwaite CW (1948) An approach towards a rational classification of climate. Geogr Rev 38:55–94

Thrasher TN, Nistal-Herrera JF, Keil LC, Ramsey DJ (1981) Satiety and inhibition of vasopressin secretion after drinking in dehydrated dogs. Am J Physiol 240: 394–401E

Tinley KL (1969) Dik-dik (*Madoqua kirkii*) in South West Africa: notes on distribution, ecology and behaviour. Madoqua 1:733

Turner JC (1984) Seasonal variation of red blood cell survival in captive and free-ranging desert bighorn sheep (*Ovis canadensis cremnobates*). Can J Zool 62:1227–1231

Vallenas A, Stevens CE (1971) Motility of the llama and guanaco stomach. Am J Physiol 220:275–282

Waites GMH, Moule GR (1961) Relation of vascular heat exchange to temperature regulation in the testis of the ram. J Reprod Fert 2:231–244

Walsberg GE, Campbell GS, King JR (1978) Animal coat colour and radiative heat gain: a reevaluation. J Comp Physiol 126B:222

Webb GJ, Johnson CR, Firth BT (1972) Head-body temperature differences in lizards. Physiol Zool 45:130–142

Williamson MAJ, Faure H (1980) The Sahara and the Nile. Quaternary environments and prehistoric occupation in northern Africa. Balkema, Rotterdam

Wilson RT (1978) The "gizu": winter grazing in the south Libyan desert. J Arid Environ 1:325–342

Wilson RT (1979) Wildlife in Southern Darfur, Sudan: Distribution and status at present and in the recent past. Mammalia 43:323–338

Wilson RT (1989) Morphology and physiology of the Hamerkop *Scopus umbretta* egg. Proc VII Pan-Afr Ornithol Cong (in press)

Wilson RT, Wilson MP (1986) Nest building by the Hamerkop, *Scopus umbretta*. Ostrich 57:224–232

Wilson RT, Wilson MP (1989) Incubation patterns of the Hamerkop *Scopus umbretta* in central Mali. Proc VI Pan-Afr Ornithol Cong 27–30

Wilson RT, Hiernaux P, McIntire J (1989) Systems studies in the Malian arid zones: research results for 1976 to 1986 (Research Report). Int Livestock Cent for Afr, Addis Ababa (in press)

Withers PC, Siegfried WR, Louw GN (1981) Desert ostrich exhales unsaturated air. S Afr J Sci 77:569–570

Yagil R (1985) The desert camel. Comparative physiological adaptation (Comparative animal nutrition, Volume 5). Karger, Basel

Yagil R, Berlyne GM (1976) Sodium and potassium metabolism in the dehydrated and hydrated camel. J Appl Physiol 41:457–461

Yagil R, Berlyne GM (1977) Glucose loading and dehydration in the camel. J Appl Physiol 42:680–683

Yagil R, Berlyne GM (1978a) Renal physiology of the dromedary camel. Nippon Jinzo Gakhai Ski 20:1015–1021

Yagil R, Berlyne GM (1978b) Glomerular filtration rate and urine concentration in the camel in dehydration. Renal Physiol 1:104–112

Yagil R, Etzion Z (1979) Antidiuretic hormone and aldosterone in the dehydrated and rehydrated camel. Comp Biochem Physiol 63A:275–278

Yagil R, Etzion Z (1980) Effect of drought condition on the quality of camel milk. J Dairy Res 47:159–166

Yagil R, Sod-Moriah UA, Meyerstein N (1974a) Dehydration and camel blood. I. The life span of the camel erythrocyte. Am J Physiol 226:298–301

Yagil R, Sod-Moriah UA, Meyerstein N (1974b) Dehydration and camel blood. II. The effect of chronic dehydration and rehydration on the shape, size and concentration of the camel red blood cell. Am J Physiol 226:301–305

Yagil R, Sod-Moriah UA, Meyerstein N (1974c) Dehydration and camel blood. III. The osmotic fragility, specific gravity and osmolality. Am J Physiol 226:305–308

Yagil R, Etzion Z, Berlyne GM (1975) Acid-base parameters in the dehydrated camel. Tijdschr Diergeneesk 100:1105–1108

Yagil R, Etzion Z, Ganani J (1978) Camel thyroid mechanism: effect of season and dehydration. J Appl Physiol 45:540–544

Yagil R, Amir H, Abu-Rabiya Y, Etzion Z (1986) Dilution of milk. A physiological adaptation of mammals to water stress? J Arid Environ 11:243–247

Yamaguchi K, Jurgens KD, Bartels H, Piiper J (1987) Oxygen transfer properties and dimensions of red blood cells in high-altitude camelids, dromedary camel and goat. J Comp Physiol 157B:1–9

Yesberg NE, Henderson M, Budtz-Olsen OE (1973) Hydration and vasopressin effects on glomerular filtration rate in sheep. Aust J Exp Biol Med Sci 51:191–197

Yousef MK, Horvath SM, Bullard RW (eds) (1972) Physiological adaptations: desert and mountain. Academic Press, London

Subject Index

DATE DUE

JAN 1 9 2001			
FEB 0 2 2002			